IN THE FOOTSTEPS OF THE
CANADIAN CORPS
CANADA'S FIRST WORLD WAR 1914–1918

Canadian War Museum   Musée canadien de la guerre

MAGIC LIGHT PUBLISHING
OTTAWA

IN THE FOOTSTEPS OF THE
CANADIAN CORPS

By: Angus Brown and Richard Gimblett
Photography: John McQuarrie

Copyright: Magic Light Publishing, 2006

Design: John McQuarrie
Cover design: David O'Malley

Published by: Magic Light Publishing
                  John McQuarrie Photography
                  192 Bruyere Street
                  Ottawa, Ontario
                  Canada   K1N 5E1
                  TEL: (613) 241-1833
                  FAX: (613) 241-2085
                  mcq@magma.ca

Library and Archives Canada Cataloguing in Publication

Brown, Angus
        In the footsteps of the Canadian Corps : Canada's First World War 1914-1918 / Angus Brown, Richard Gimblett ; photographs by John McQuarrie.

Includes bibliographical references and index.
ISBN 1-894673-24-7 (soft-cover edition)
ISBN 1-894673-28-X (hard-cover edition)

        1. Canada. Canadian Army--History--World War, 1914-1918. 2. Canada. Canadian Army--History--World War, 1914-1918--Pictorial works. 3. World War, 1914-1918--Battlefields--Pictorial works. I. Gimblett, Richard Howard, 1956-II. McQuarrie, John, 1946- III. Title

D547.C2B76 2006   940.41'271   C2006-900304-1

Printed in Canada

Acknowledgements

We had a lot of fun putting this book together, but we also had a lot of help.   Foremost, our thanks must go to our former Governor General, the Right Honourable Adrienne Clarkson, for agreeing to write the foreword. The Canadian War Museum (CWM) staff have been of great assistance. Dennis Fletcher, Maggie Arbour-Doucette and Laura Brandon provided invaluable advice and rapid response for the bulk of the imagery. Dr Dean Oliver was supportive in the production process of the book. The Directorate of History and Heritage at the Department of National Defence (DND) graciously consented to the use of maps from the official histories. Photos were also provided by Pepper Mintz, the Rosetown Centennial Library Archive, Saskatchewan, Library and Archives Canada (NAC), Corporal Isabel Paré, Bill Constable, Manon Lévis, and Steve Douglas. Barbara Brown of the Canadian Broadcasting Corporation (CBC) Archives added an interesting element to the project with the "In Flanders Fields" radio series. Our thanks go out to all, but the responsibility for errors, omissions or inaccuracies remains with us.

Select Bibliography

Rose E.B. Coombs, Before Endeavours Fade: A Guide to the Battlefields of the First World War
        (London: Battle of Britain International Ltd, 1998 [eighth printing]).
D.J. Goodspeed, The Road Past Vimy: The Canadian Corps, 1914-1918 (Toronto: Macmillan, 1969).
Desmond Morton and J.L. Granatstein, Marching to Armageddon: Canadians and the Great War, 1914-1919
        (Toronto: Lester and Orpen Dennys, 1989).
G.W.L. Nicholson, Canadian Expeditionary Force, 1914-1919 (Ottawa: Queen's Printer, 1964). Note: this out-of-print
        title is available on-line at the "Publications" link of the Directorate of History and Heritage website below.
Dean Oliver and Laura Brandon, Canvas of War: Painting the Canadian Experience, 1914 to 1945 (Vancouver &
        Toronto: Douglas & McIntyre, 2000).
G. Kingsley Ward and Major Edwin Gibson, Courage Remembered: The Story Behind the Construction and Maintenance
        of the Military Cemeteries and Memorials of the Wars of 1914-1918 and 1939-1945
        (Toronto: McClelland & Stewart, 1989).
Jonathan F. Vance, Death So Noble: Memory, Meaning, and the First World War (Vancouver: UBC Press, 1997).

Websites referred to in this book:
Canadian War Museum: http://www.warmuseum.ca
Commonwealth War Graves Commission: http://www.cwgc.org
Directorate of History and Heritage: http://www.dnd.ca/dhh/engraph/home_e.asp
Library and Archives Canada: http://www.collectionscanada.ca/archivianet/020106_e.html
Maple leaf Legacy Project: http://www.mapleleaflegacy.org
Veterans Affairs Canada: http://www.vac-acc.gc.ca/remembers/

To purchase a copy or find out more information about the CBC-produced radio series "In Flanders Fields"
call 1-800-955-7711 or order online at www.cbcshop.ca

TABLE OF CONTENTS

MEMORIAL
REGISTER

FOREWORD

To learn about the role of the Canadian Corps during the First World War is to be plunged into the violent forging of the metal of our country. This war left its searing marks on the thousands of families of wounded or dead soldiers. It is a bitter legacy of what a hideous human price is paid by those who are thrown into the maelstrom of conflict not created by them - the brave, the innocent, the confused, the obedient.

This book gives a visual and verbal texture to that horror, to what it meant to be part of the carnage. It was the first modern war: in Sir Alfred Munning's "Charge of Flowerdew's Squadron" we see the old world of battle and the new together in a hallucinatory timeless way.

All the battles with the filthy water-logged trenches, the barbed wire, are here. The group portrait of the Canadian Headquarters Staff meticulously uniformed, carefully avoiding the viewer's and each other's eyes, tells more about the hollow terror of this war than any words. It was a war in which a young Major Vanier, later Governor General of Canada, lost his leg in a battle in which purportedly all the officers were either killed or wounded. It is a war we will always see because the war artists like F. H. Varley and A.Y. Jackson have created a vision of beauty out of destruction. It is a war to whose heart, soul and guts this book takes us.

We must never forget our history because we must never lose our memory. Collectively, we, as a people, need our memory to remember our past, to live in the present, and not stumble into the future.

All through the history of our country we have lurched and lunged through a forest of ignorance and apathy, hacking ourselves a path which can only remain a clearing if we maintain it, if we agree to enlarge it, and promise ourselves and pledge to each other that it is worth our efforts.

The Canadian Corps, by its willing sacrifice, helped us to keep that lighted space.

The Right Honourable Adrienne Clarkson, PC, CC, CMM, CD
Governor General of Canada and Commander-in-Chief 1999-2005

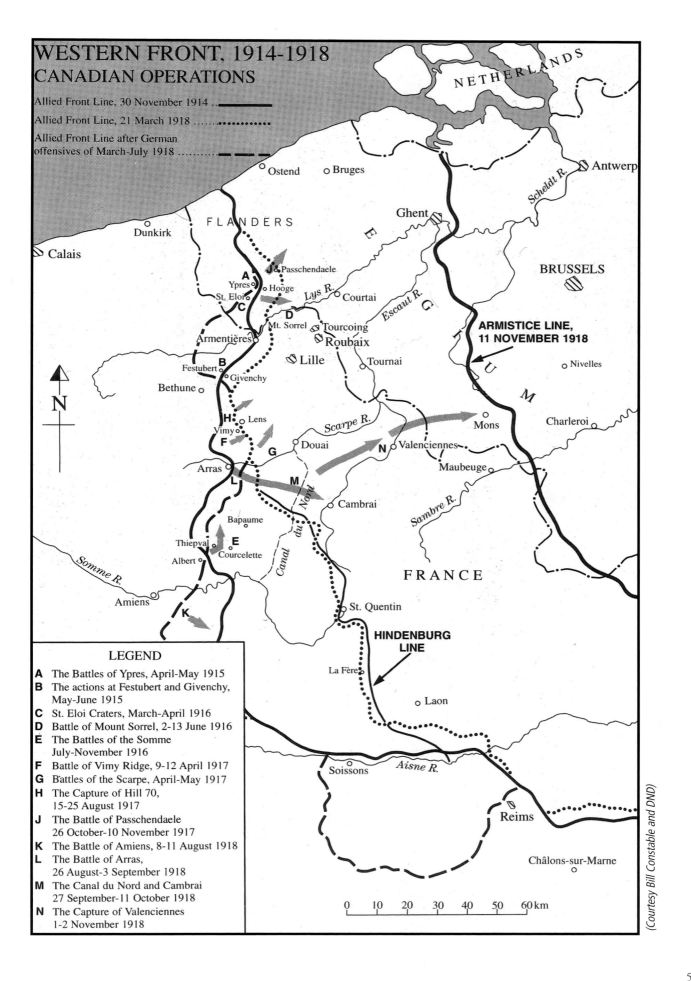

WESTERN FRONT, 1914-1918
CANADIAN OPERATIONS

Allied Front Line, 30 November 1914 . . . _____

Allied Front Line, 21 March 1918 . . . . . . ●●●●●●●●

Allied Front Line after German
offensives of March-July 1918 . . . . ━ ━ ━

NETHERLANDS

Ostend   Bruges   Antwerp
Scheldt R.

Calais   Dunkirk   FLANDERS   Ghent   BRUSSELS

J Passchendaele
A   Ypres   Hooge
St. Eloi   Lys R.   Courtai
C   D   Escaut R.
Mt. Sorrel   Tourcoing   ARMISTICE LINE,
Armentières   Roubaix   11 NOVEMBER 1918
B   Lille   Tournai   Nivelles
Festubert   Givenchy
Bethune   Charleroi
H   Lens
Vimy   Scarpe R.   Mons
F   Douai   N   Valenciennes
G   Maubeuge
Arras   M
L   Sambre R.
Bapaume   Cambrai
Thiepval   E
Albert   Courcelette   Canal du Nord   FRANCE
Somme R.
Amiens   St. Quentin
K   HINDENBURG
LINE
La Fère
Laon

Soissons   Aisne R.

Reims

Châlons-sur-Marne

N

0 10 20 30 40 50 60 km

LEGEND

A The Battles of Ypres, April-May 1915
B The actions at Festubert and Givenchy,
   May-June 1915
C St. Eloi Craters, March-April 1916
D Battle of Mount Sorrel, 2-13 June 1916
E The Battles of the Somme
   July-November 1916
F Battle of Vimy Ridge, 9-12 April 1917
G Battles of the Scarpe, April-May 1917
H The Capture of Hill 70,
   15-25 August 1917
J The Battle of Passchendaele
   26 October-10 November 1917
K The Battle of Amiens, 8-11 August 1918
L The Battle of Arras,
   26 August-3 September 1918
M The Canal du Nord and Cambrai
   27 September-11 October 1918
N The Capture of Valenciennes
   1-2 November 1918

(Courtesy Bill Constable and DND)

William Longstaff, "The Ghosts of Vimy" (CWM, 19860331-018)

Mopping up on Vimy Ridge, 9 April 1917. (CWM, CEF Album 2, 1155)

INTRODUCTION

The First World War is now a memory.   The people who experienced it, fought in it, and who had firsthand recollection of that time and era are now gone. Many Canadians, however, still have a connection to the Great War through memorabilia, family keepsakes and genealogical ties.

On a national historical level, the First World War is extremely important for Canada. It is an accepted fact that Canada "became a nation" during the conflict as a result of the immense effort the country put forth. Symbolically, Vimy Ridge is often cited as the seminal event of Canadian nationhood.   Practically, however, the complete 1914-1919 war experience was a turning point for the colony that became a country.

While the people who made history have passed from the scene, a rich legacy remains. It touches most Canadians on an almost daily basis. Nearly every town and city across the country has at least one cenotaph or statue dedicated to the memory of those who fought and died in the war.   Churches, schools and public buildings have bronze plaques and stained glass windows in memory of citizens, or more often their sons, who failed to return home. The National War Memorial in Ottawa was inspired by the sacrifices of those who fought in the First World War. Books of Remembrance are kept and displayed in the Parliament Buildings and are available on the Internet. The iconic Peace Tower that anchors the Centre Block, originally referred to by some as the "Victory Tower", was built specifically to commemorate the end of the war to end all wars. One of the most historically important art collections in the nation is held at the Canadian War Museum and reflects the efforts of Canadians in the Great War.

But some of the largest and most striking physical memorials to Canadian military history are not even in the country.   They are in Europe. After the war, a series of memorials was erected at important places where Canadians fought.   Partly this was a reflection of the tenor of the times: practically every country that participated erected memorials on the battlefields where their sons fell.

However, the discerning visitor is left with the vague but undeniable feeling that the Canadian memorials are somehow grander in scale and scope than one might logically consider they should be, given the size of Canada at the time, barely eight million in population. Indeed, most of those memorials dwarf almost anything found in the average city in Canada. Some of them - Vimy Ridge leaps to mind - are among the most impressive to be found in Northwest Europe.

The tragedy is that many Canadians will never see these memorials simply because they are in Europe. Even those lucky enough to tour France and Belgium may not see them because the memorials are often in out of the way places, off the beaten track, on the sites of the battles. One normally has to make a special effort to visit them and, in some places, one has to actively seek them out.   For those who do take the time and make the effort, the memorials raise more questions than answers. What happened here? How did that event fit into the grand scheme of things? Why were those people of another generation so moved that they felt the need to spend all this money and time to commemorate Canadian deeds in a far-off land? Who were they, these people who traveled so far, too many of them never to return to the country that sent them off to fight?

Unlike other wars in other places - the American Civil War, for instance - only a few of the European battlefields, or segments of them, have been preserved or maintained. The European memorials are unique to a time and place. They reflect not only the fashion of the times but the determination of a generation to pay homage to their own contemporaries' deeds, and to leave a tangible, obvious memory for future generations. We are those future generations.

This book is part history, part travelogue and part memory.   Through its pages, the reader can follow in the footsteps of the Canadian Expeditionary Force, primarily the Canadian Corps, the premier Canadian army fighting formation during the war. Through the medium of text, art and photos, it explores where Canadian soldiers went during the First World War and what they did.

The Vimy Memorial today dominates the scene of the battle. (Photo: Pepper Mintz)

All of the art and most of the archival photos are taken from the collections of the Canadian War Museum. Modern photos try to mimic the scenes as much as possible. In doing so the intent is first to show what occurred, then to describe some of the context in which the events transpired, and finally to see how the area looks today.

The contrasts are stark. Ruined towns are now prosperous cities, some of them having endured a second destruction and yet another reincarnation after the Second World War.   Many have been reconstructed faithfully in the previous style while others have become examples of modern architecture. Pastoral farmland now replaces the killing grounds of mud and wire and trenches. Where pitched battles raged, quiet, meditative memorials now remain.

Many of the pictures show people. These were our grandparents, our great uncles or aunts. They are not the jerky, scratchy, grainy, toy-like characters that flit across our video screens in old movies or documentary films. Look at the faces and you will see earnest young men, pretty young women and a few children. The faces are those of common people doing extraordinary things that were beyond the comprehension of most of them only months before the pictures were snapped. They were tired, elated, dirty, cleaned up for a portrait, homesick, casual or determined. They were how we see ourselves today, only a generation or two removed. They were reflections of us but in their own time. They all were Canadians, or came to regard themselves as Canadians, because of their wartime experience.

The Canadian Corps was the clearest manifestation of this surging nationality. In its ranks were people from all walks of life and all corners of the country.   While many units began as regional, almost tribal groupings in some cases, individual members soon became very aware of Canadians in other units as they served and fought together. Often individuals were mixed up and found themselves sharing comfort and danger with people from parts of Canada that had only been distant names to them. Immigrants and native-born Canadians found their membership in the Canadian Corps to be a unifying experience.

There are three constant and intertwined factors on any battlefield, in any war. They are: technology, tactics and terrain. Each one affects the other two and usually triggers changes in them. The changes can become circular as one change begets another. For instance, the advent of the machinegun and quick-firing artillery (technology) brought about a change to the way war was practised. No longer were cavalry charges and extended lines of infantry (the tactics of earlier times) feasible. Trenches became the only way to survive, but this (a change in the terrain) meant that there had to be a solution sought in technology to overcome the changed terrain. Hence, the tank, aircraft and complex artillery procedures were developed. The Canadian Corps, founded upon a base of untrained volunteer soldiers, had to master all of the "three Ts" while at the same time learning its basic warfighting skills.

The Canadian Corps, of course, did not win the war alone. It was only one of many formations that took its turn in the battleground that was the Western Front. However, it was unique in number of ways. Its organization was relatively constant, unlike other British Empire formations that were broken up or parcelled out piecemeal to meet emergencies of the day. This allowed the Canadian Corps to form an esprit that contributed to its efficiency. It was also well-equipped and big in relation to other equivalent army formations. The Canadian Corps did not follow the British practice in the latter part of the war of re-organizing itself to produce more but weaker units. The Corps stressed technical advancement and pioneered improvements in artillery and engineer employment and tactics. The Canadian Corps thus became a force to be reckoned with and was tracked carefully by enemy intelligence officers.

Today it is possible for all Canadians to track the progress and achievements of the Canadian Corps across France and Belgium by following the trail of memorials. There is certainly more to the story than Vimy Ridge. Our ancestors accomplished much and built those memorials to record their achievements. We owe it to their memory to commemorate - and to celebrate - that their comrades did not die in vain.

C.W. Jefferys, "Observation Post, Petawawa" (CWM, 19710261-0211)

THE WORLD TURNS UPSIDE DOWN

28th Battalion leaving Winnipeg, May 28th, 1915, and the Winnipeg rail yards today. (CWM 19640037-018, and Richard Gimblett)

When war erupted in Europe in early August of 1914, there was no Canadian Corps. Indeed, there was not much of a military establishment at all in Canada. The miniscule Militia was nothing resembling an army. It was far removed from an efficient organization that could train recruits, form specialist units, cross a major ocean, fight against the leading military power of the day, and carve out a place for itself as the pre-eminent fighting formation on the Western Front in a "war to end all wars".

What Canada did have was a loosely organized group of military units spread across the country numbering about 59,000 men. In many cases, these local Militia units were more social than military and almost all were under-strength and under-equipped. There was, however, a small cadre of officers and non-commissioned officers (NCOs), some with previous military campaign experience, mostly in the Boer War. The total regular armed forces, including a small newly formed naval complement, numbered only about 3,000 souls. Their main job was to provide training for the Militia units. A number of individuals, both regular and reserve, took their training seriously and diligently qualified themselves in accordance with the training requirements of the day, all of which were derived from the British War Office.

A small headquarters in Ottawa, headed by a professional British officer and staffed mainly with British officers seconded to Canada, did administration and planning as was required. Most of the operational planning was derived from the directives of the British War Office and British Admiralty. When Britain declared war on Germany on 4 August 1914, it was axiomatic that Canada, a self-governing Dominion but staunch member of the British Empire, was at war also. Canada had no war aims other than to help the Empire and Mother Country, Great Britain.

There was a Canadian military mobilization plan and, in early 1914, an inter-departmental committee had drawn up plans for general governmental actions in case of war. In the event, the eccentric and mercurial

Minister of Militia and Defence, Sam Hughes, ignored or countermanded most of the plans. Instead of the orderly muster and dispatch of the Militia, almost immediately upon the declaration of war Hughes offered a force of 20,000 to 25,000 Canadian volunteers for service with Britain's army. Hughes decreed that units across the country should begin to recruit and send people to Camp Valcartier just north of Quebec City. Unfortunately, there was no military base there and troops arriving found that their first job was to build the camp on the sandy waste ground.

The tenor of the times was thus set. Hughes rampaged throughout the bureaucracy and excitedly micro-managed the call to arms, issuing orders down to the lowest levels, while creating confusion at higher levels by impinging upon the responsibility of other government departments. Order, counter-order and disorder were the characteristics of the time due to the erratic and meddling ways of the Minister. Procurement of supplies was a monumental task and the hand of Hughes was everywhere ensuring contracts went to his friends and government allies. He had already had a great influence on the adoption of the soon-to-be infamous Ross rifle for the Militia; other even wilder schemes, such as the entrenching tool with a hole in it to allow it to be used as a shooting shield, came quickly to the fore. Behind Hughes, valiantly trying to piece together a semblance of an army organization, came the small and completely overworked military staff.

Rosetown volunteers waiting for their uniforms,1914; and uniforms have arrived (right). (Courtesy Rosetown Centennial Library Archive)

96th Battalion passing in review before Brigadier-General J. Hughes, 12 April 1916, Camp Hughes . (Courtesy Rosetown Centennial Library Archive)

The excitement and patriotic fervour evident in these photographs taken at Rosetown, Saskatchewan were repeated in hundreds of towns and cities across Canada. Peer pressure played a major part in recruiting. Almost every community now has a cenotaph or memorial in a public place to remember those that did not return.

War Memorial, Rosetown.
(Courtesy Dorothy J. Seibold)

Leaving Rosetown, August 1914. (CWM, 19810649-028) (Below) "Decoration Day", Rosetown.

(Courtesy Rosetown Centennial Library Archive)

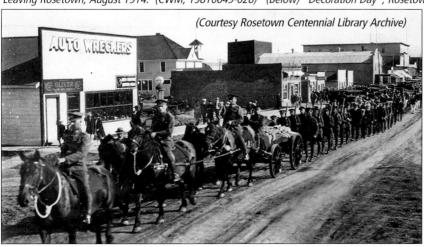

Aerial view of Canadian Forces Base Valacartier today. (DND Photo)

The modern day Canadian Forces Base Valcartier (top left) has undergone many changes since 1914. When Sam Hughes decided to concentrate troops there in 1914, it was because of the proximity to the port of Quebec City and not because of the facilities. In fact, there was almost nothing at Valcartier in 1914 and the initial job of the troops sent there was to provide much of the labour to construct camps. One of Hughes' concerns was to get the Canadians on ships and over to England before winter struck the mainly tented camp.

Camp Hughes in Manitoba was another of the training areas set up across the Dominion to handle recruits and some mobilized Militia units. For the most part, these locales had only been used for summer training of small units. They were tented and, like Valcartier, much work was necessary to make them effective training areas. The location of Camp Hughes is now a provincial recreation area and only a small marker denotes its military heritage.

Camp Hughes., Manitoba . (CWM, 19940027-069)

*"Whether we liked Sam Hughes or no,
somebody certainly did a lot of engineering there."*
B.C. Lunn, 16th Battalion
CBC Radio, In Flanders Fields
Episode 2, "Canada Answers the Call"

Valcartier was a sea of bell tents. The camp was hewn from the wilderness, often by the troops sent there to train. (CWM, J-5 19810649-030, p. 2)

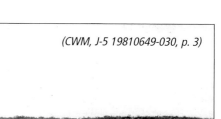

Troops on rifle range in Valcartier.

Troops at morning ablutions.

Troops at Camp Hughes in Manitoba (below) also lived in tented camps.

Quebec City today with the Citadel, and the waterfront dominated by the Chateau Frontenac.

(CWM, J-5 19810649-030, p. 10)

The First Contingent convoy sails from Quebec City.

"Our ocean voyage began on the third of October and our first day out was very rough, and as most of our boys had done all their deep sea sailoring on the Red River, we thought it was very fortunate that we had the medical staff and plenty of nurses on board. ... It was a very impressive scene when all the ships were steaming along three abreast and stretched out for many miles, surrounded by British Cruisers and destroyers, and one saw how wonderful the British Navy was, to be able to transport such a large body of men in safety, and one had the feeling of security aboard when one looked around and saw those speedy little destroyers on all sides always on the alert for signs of the 'Hun' submarine."
Fred Fraser, 90th Winnipeg Rifles

Private Memoir (author's collection)

F.S. Challener, "Canada's Grand Armada" (CWM 19710261-0120)

Lieutenant-Commander Norman Wilkinson, "Canada's Answer": the First Contingent convoy in formation off Gaspe. (CWM 19710261-0791)

"We couldn't see where anybody could knock the British Lion off the map at all."
Victor Lewis, 4th Battalion
CBC Radio, In Flanders Fields
Episode 2, "Canada Answers the Call"

Bayonet practice, somewhere in England. (CWM, CEF Album 7, M295B)

One of Hughes' most contentious decisions was to scrap the existing regimental organizations and to put the drafts of recruits and militiamen alike into numbered battalions in numbered brigades within a divisional structure. The Militia felt betrayed and soldiers were bewildered, belonging one day to a proud and historical unit and the next being part of a faceless polyglot creation of a unit. Eventually, over the course of the war, these battalions themselves assumed regional or unit titles, often expressed in brackets behind their battalion number, in response to the desire of their members to be part of more than an anonymous grouping of lost souls.

One unit, the Princess Patricia's Canadian Light Infantry (the PPCLI), was raised by the wealthy Hamilton Gault and consisted of mainly men with former British Army service. With such a high number of veterans, the unit was ready for employment before all others. It joined the British Expeditionary Force (BEF) on the continent ahead of all other Canadian units and fought as part of the English forces for almost a year. Later in the war some other units were raised through the auspices of other wealthy businessmen or organizations. The Eaton family, for instance, financed a machine gun battery and various universities contributed medical staff for some field ambulance units.

Training of the Canadian volunteers at Valcartier, and a number of other centres set up across the country, was rudimentary. When the troops were not engaged in tending to the basics of creature comforts, they lined up for standard issues of equipment, clothing and weapons, and set about mastering the most elementary of military manouevres. Route marches were frequent and great store was placed upon marksmanship. There were endless hours spent sorting out organizations, people, kit, baggage, wagons, horses and guns. Over 30,000 men reported to Valcartier alone and about 5,000 of them were almost immediately culled from the ranks as being unfit, undesirable or unsuitable for one reason or the other.

Hughes planned to send the first contingent of Canadians to England within weeks. So hasty was he that there was a rather sharp procession of telegrams from the Admiralty ordering the Canadians not to move until proper convoy escort could be arranged across the Atlantic. The actual loading of ships at Quebec was reflective of the hurried and unprofessional shambles that was transpiring with the First Contingent, as it was now known. Lack of planning and with no proper movement control staff to supervise the operation meant that some ships sailed only half full and others were stuffed to the gunwhales. Some units began boarding men and horses on 23 September and all stowage on board the 30 ships going in the convoy was completed, with a high degree of chaos, by the evening of 1 October. They sailed the next day, with a Royal Navy escort of battleships and cruisers, and screened by other elements of the Grand Fleet (the newly-formed Royal Canadian Navy did not have any ships capable of joining the effort), a scene famously captured in the painting "Canada's Answer".

One ship, the *Manhattan*, finished loading on 5 October, with bits and pieces the others forgot or could not fit into their holds, and sailed independently from Quebec to Southampton. The official report of the officer charged with loading the ships makes for interesting reading. He indicated that the loading manifests were probably incorrect and some items were missing, including almost 400 bicycles!

For what they were worth, those manifests showed some 30,617 officers and men, 7,679 horses (both riding and draft), 70 pieces of artillery, 110 motorized vehicles and 705 wagons were on their way to England and war. The large convoy steamed down the St Lawrence and was met en route by two other ships, one at Gaspé Bay coming from Bermuda with a British regiment and another off Newfoundland with a contingent of that colony's contribution to the war effort, the Royal Newfoundland Regiment.

SALISBURY PLAIN

"Why anybody survived that winter on the plains, I don't know. Mud everywhere, rain all the time."
Ian Sinclair, 16th Battalion
CBC Radio, In Flanders Fields
Episode 3, "The Great Expedition"

Canadian troops endured bad weather, sickness and extensive flooding at Salisbury Plain in England, 1915. (CWM, CEF Album 4, M316)

The convoy steamed uneventfully across the Atlantic, the only alarm arising near the UK coast when a German submarine was sighted off the Isle of Wight. Because of congestion and defensive concerns, the convoy was diverted from its planned destination of Liverpool and arrived in Plymouth on the morning of 14 October 1914.

Disembarkation took almost a week as the troops and their officers sorted out the equipment, horses, vehicles and weapons on the ships that unloaded in turn. The hurried and disorganized embarkation in Quebec meant that some items of a particular unit's equipment were found loaded in a number of different ships. Then it transpired that units were being sent to different localities in the Salisbury Plain area of southern England and confusion deepened. Notwithstanding all that, most Canadians had taken up residence in English army camps by 22 October.

Hughes had wanted to get the Canadian soldiers to the UK as soon as possible, mostly out of a desire to get troops "over there" as soon as possible, but partly also because of the problems an approaching Canadian winter posed for a Valcartier camp still under construction. These difficulties were not avoided, however, as new, similar problems soon arose in England. First, the weather turned bad: the Canadians experienced some of the wettest autumn weather ever seen on Salisbury Plain.

Then, it became clear that accommodation was a problem in England, too. Camps suffered from flooding and soldiers remembered for many years afterward that they seldom remained dry or warm for long. Sickness rates began to rise and various illnesses swept through whole units, delaying training. Being wet and cold abroad was almost as bad for the soldiers as being just plain cold at home.

Canadian equipment was soon determined to be either inferior or non-standard. Boots were not durable. Wagons and harness equipment were incompatible with spares and replacement parts in use elsewhere in the British army. The Canadians had to be re-equipped wholesale, much to the chagrin of Hughes.

The training bore little resemblance to the realities of what awaited them. (CWM, J-5 19810649-030, p. 21)

The training that was done, while better than the elementary instruction in Canada, was not always terribly useful, as the Canadian Division would discover when it arrived on the Continent. In this regard, however, the Canadians were no different from the rest of the British Army, which itself was learning the intricacies of the new type of trench warfare. Everyone, friend and foe alike, was in a steep learning curve.

The Canadian Division, as it was now being organized and called, was placed under the command of an experienced British officer, Major General E.A.H. Alderson. This was only the beginning. The Dominion government already had offered another 20,000 men to Britain, and committed to filling any replacements needed to take the place of the casualties. The Second Contingent also would be organized along the lines of a division. With supporting troops, base units in the UK and in France, and replacements continually flowing into the theatre, Canada's huge contribution of manpower eventually would swell to a large four-division army corps.

Lieutenant Alfred Theodore Joseph Bastien, "Gas Attack, Flanders, 1915" (CWM, 19710261-0084)

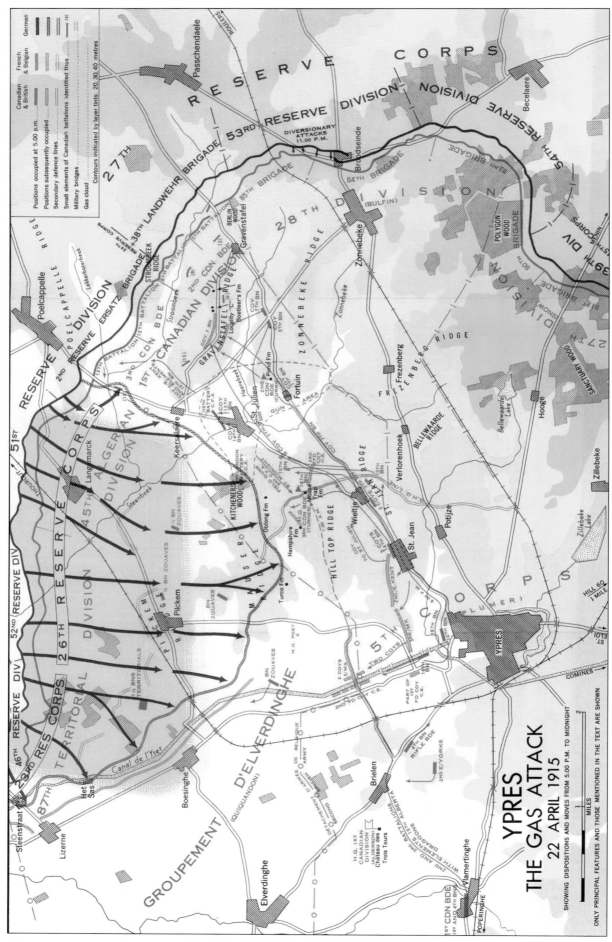

**YPRES
THE GAS ATTACK
22 APRIL 1915**

SHOWING DISPOSITIONS AND MOVES FROM 5.00 P.M. TO MIDNIGHT

ONLY PRINCIPAL FEATURES AND THOSE MENTIONED IN THE TEXT ARE SHOWN

MILES
1   0   1   2

Positions occupied at 5.00 p.m.
Positions subsequently occupied
Secondary defence lines
Small elements of Canadian battalions identified thus
Military bridges
Gas cloud

German
French & Belgian
Canadian & British

Contours indicated by layer tints: 20, 30, 40 metres

(Courtesy DND Directorate of History and Heritage)

22

Into the Salient

These soldiers from the 22nd Battalion, later the Royal 22e Regiment - theVan Doos - have adapted to life in the trenches. (CWM, CEF Album 1, 0272)

After crossing the Channel and landing in St Nazaire in mid-February 1915, the Canadian Division moved by rail to the area of Hazebrouk, southwest of Ypres in Belgium, where it went into a reserve position. The officers and men of the division now set about becoming familiar with the characteristics of the real battlefield, not the stylized training scenarios they had practiced in England. Individually and in groups of small units, Canadian battalions and brigades were successively introduced to trench routine and life in the front lines by the simple expediency of accompanying units of the British Expeditionary Force that were manning the forward positions.

By the end of February, the Canadian Division was declared to be operationally ready and was given the task of relieving the British 7th Division in a sector near Fleurbaix, just over the border into France, as part of 4th British Corps. Responsible for over 6,000 yards of the front south of Armentières, the Canadians were charged with defensive operations. General Alderson ordered aggressive patrolling and sniper activity so that the division would dominate No Man's Land.

During March, the Canadian Division artillery supported the British offensive in the area of Neuve Chapelle (10-12 March) and, at one time, it appeared that the Canadians might be committed to exploit some gains. The British assault was not successful, however, because of communications difficulties and strong German resistance, and the Canadian Division did not advance from their trenches.

Eventually, as a result of a general northward re-deployment of the BEF into the Ypres salient in Belgium to relieve French Army troops there, the Canadian Division was placed under command of the 5th Corps in Second British Army.   Over the first week in April, the Division physically moved to the north to the area of Cassel, a small town about 20 km west of Ypres, to begin training to move into new positions.

Ypres was the scene of bitter fighting throughout the war and the fact it was referred to as a "salient" gives some explanation as to why. In simple terms, a salient is a bulge of friendly lines into enemy territory. During the initial German advance in 1914, their cavalry patrols penetrated into the city proper and beyond. As the line settled into trench warfare, the Germans withdrew to establish their main defensive positions on the ridges that circled Ypres to the north, east and southeast.

Dominating the high ground, the Germans built strong defensive positions and settled in for the long term, determined to retain the initiative. Allied units had to endure constant observation and the inevitable artillery and machinegun fire that came with it, but did not feel that they could abandon the city for a host of military and political reasons. The Ypres Salient remained a dangerous place throughout the war, and the city was for all practical purposes obliterated. In fact, such a situation was repeated in several places along the Western Front, and in each instance those locations inevitably became a focal point for prolonged and intense fighting. It was a common refrain among Allied soldiers that they were always attacking uphill against a well-entrenched enemy.

Main photo Steve Douglas; inset Rose Coombs, Before Endeavours Fade.

The almost total devastation by enemy shelling of the city of Ypres in Belgium, known to most Empire soldiers as "Wipers" and today by its Flemish name of Ieper, was symbolic of the Western Front for British and Empire troops. The city was designed as a Vauban fortress complete with major moat and ramparts. German cavalry penetrated to the west of the city in August 1914, before withdrawing to the north, east and south of Ypres when the British Expeditionary Force counter-attacked. Throughout 1915 to 1917, two more major battles, and many smaller actions, were fought in the area. Units had to negotiate crossing points over the Yser Canal there and major roads led via the town towards the front. Because enemy forces occupied high ground generally overlooking Ypres, the city was systematically reduced to rubble as artillery sought out Allied troop movements and concentrations.

Reconstruction began shortly after the Armistice in 1918. The city was spared major damage in the Second World War and was liberated from German occupation by the Polish Armoured Division, part of First Canadian Army, in September 1944. The city is a major destination for military tourists interested in the Western Front.

LILLE GATE

Ypres is an old fortified, walled city. Over many years and many wars the ramparts and the fortifications have been pressed into service. Ypres has also been a transportation hub, a site of manufacturing and the centre of rural farmland. In the Great War, Ypres was an important gateway to the defensive positions of the salient facing the surrounding ridges. Troops moved into and out of their positions via the road and rail network in the city.

The city itself contained numerous headquarters and logistical installations, often burrowed into the thick medieval walls. The Lille Gate was one of the main routes into and out of the city from the military rear areas. The railway station was nearby and the main road network branched out from here to a myriad of old and new roads and tracks. The water is part of the former moat that surrounded the city and joined, in former times, to the Yser Canal.

The city took a terrible pounding over the war years, seldom being out of range of German artillery of many different calibres. The picture below shows the damage caused by repeated artillery strikes.

Today a modern ring road allows traffic to bypass the old city and connects to a high-speed autoroute that skirts to the north. Near this gate is the main modern-day railway station and, during the war, there were smaller narrow gauge railways throughout this area. Just to the left of this picture, inside the gate, is the Ramparts Commonwealth War Graves Cemetery, one of a number in and around the city limits. Inside the city, streets are still fairly narrow and typical of the original medieval city plan. Along the ramparts today is a beautiful park. Children now play and families stroll where soldiers of many centuries lived and died.

(CWM, CEF Album 6, 4683)

YPRES

> "The Cloth Hall had been shelled but not to a great extent, and then the Germans began suddenly shelling the town square. And people were screaming and running hither and thither."
>
> N. Nicholson, 16th Battalion
> *CBC Radio, In Flanders Fields*
> Episode 5, "The Second Battle of Ypres"

(This page) Canadian soldiers examine the ruins of the Cloth Hall from the main square in Ypres. (CWM, CEF Album 1, 0449)

(Opposite bottom right) The ruins of St Martin's Cathedral through an arch of the Cloth Hall. (CWM, CEF Album 3, 2156)

The Cloth Hall and neighbouring St Martin's Cathedral both suffered massive damage from artillery bombardment of the city of Ypres during the Great War. The Cloth Hall, dating from the 13th century, had been a centre of the textile trade in Europe and ships once came to its doors via a canal that linked the city with the Channel ports. The canal was long ago filled in but the Cloth Hall remained as a jewel of secular architechture in the French Gothic style. St Martin's, with its flying buttresses and spectacular stained glass windows, was also a landmark.

Some people, among them Winston Chuchill, suggested that the ruined Ypres be left as a memorial to the folly of war. However, the Belgian people were determined to rebuild and the city centre was returned to its former glory, the final restoration of the Cloth Hall being completed in the early 1960s. It is now a concert hall and the site of the In Flanders Fields Museum.

VANCOUVER CORNER

Vancouver Corner today.

Today, as one drives northeast from the city of Ypres past St Jean to the vicinity of St Julien, the large Canadian monument commonly called the "Brooding Soldier" comes into view at the next intersection. This memorial marks Canadian participation in the Second Battle of Ypres. It was constructed in the locality known in 1915 as Vancouver Corner, photographed here in 1917. (CWM, CEF Album 6, 4653)

THE BROODING SOLDIER

CANADA

THIS·COLUMN·MARKS·THE
BATTLEFIELD·WHERE·18,000
CANADIANS·ON·THE·BRITISH
LEFT·WITHSTOOD·THE·FIRST
GERMAN·GAS·ATTACKS·THE
22-24·APRIL·1915·2,000·FELL
AND·LIE·BURIED·NEARBY

In mid-April, the Canadians moved into positions formerly occupied by French troops northeast of the city of Ypres near St Julien. French infantry still manned the line to their left. The French-British inter-army boundary ran approximately along the road from Ypres to Poelkappele, the latter held by the Germans, with the area to the north of the road being the responsibility of the French Army. Two Canadian brigades were deployed over a distance of about 4500 yards, forward of the ridge at Gravenstafel, in a crescent to the southeast. Each brigade in the line had two battalions forward and one back, a normal deployment, the entire division being supported by British troops to their rear and on the southeastern flank. Except for a brigade located deep in reserve west of Ypres (for all practical purposes out of the battle area and, in fact, warned for employment in another sector) the Canadian Division had all its strength "in the shop window."

This Second Battle of Ypres was important for two reasons. First, of course, the engagements in that area in the time frame 22-27 April 1915 were the initial major battles fought by Canadians in Europe. Secondly, it was notable for the fact that the German army used gas as a weapon, not for the very first time but to stunning effect on a large scale.

German army chemical engineers judged wind conditions to be suitable in the late afternoon of 22 April. In concert with a sharp artillery bombardment along both the French and Canadian positions, they opened the valves on almost 6,000 cannisters of chlorine gas. Over 160 tons of gas formed a green cloud and was picked up by light northeast winds blowing primarily over the French positions to the left of the Canadian trenches.

The situation developed quickly and seriously. French troops were overwhelmed by the gas and moved back, or died where they stood from the choking effects of the chlorine and the accompanying artillery and small arms fire. Although the Canadians had escaped the effects of the initial chemical attack, the rout of their allies on the northern flank west of St Julien left them exposed. More dramatically, the way to Ypres was rapidly opening up to the Germans, to the point that rear area troops began to prepare crossings over the Yser Canal for demolition. The city and the remaining British divisions holding the salient were now seriously threatened.

The Canadian Division's battalions and brigades hurriedly moved forces to their left and took advancing German units under fire with both artillery and small arms. The First Brigade and other British units from the rear were desperately dispatched to plug the hole that was developing in the front line north of Ypres. Because of confusion and communications difficulties, brigade and battalion commanders found that they had to act on their own initiative without the benefit of good intelligence or higher direction.

By morning of 23 April, the German 52nd Division had pushed a bulge into the Allied lines that stretched as far as the Yser Canal west of Pilckem to the area west of St Julien and down south to about one mile from the Ypres-Poelkappele road. Canadian and British and some French units launched counter-attacks by night and day to stem the surging tide of German field gray uniforms.

In an attempt to eliminate or reduce the Ypres Salient, the Germans launched another gas attack on the morning of 24 April, this time directly against the Canadian positions. Desperate fighting to the east and northwest of St Julien ensued. Through the day and the following night into the 25th, Canadian Division units were pushed back slowly by a preponderance of artillery, gas and infantry attacks.

It was here that a Canadian medical officer with knowledge of chemistry devised the expedient of having his troops cover their faces with urine-soaked handkerchiefs to mitigate the effects of the chlorine gas clouds. Later in this action, that same officer won the Victoria Cross for saving and protecting the wounded.

Over the course of the 25th of April, St Julien was lost, as was most of the ridge to the east. Eventually, the exhausted Canadians were pulled from the line on 26 April and replaced. The German advance was stemmed and the line eventually was stabilized by French, British and Indian Army counterattacks on 27 April. Fighting continued, however, with both German and Allied local offensives until early May.

While all this was occurring, the Princess Patricia's Canadian Light Infantry (the PPCLI) had still been attached to the 80th Brigade of the 27th British Division only a relatively short distance to the south. In early May, as part of their parent formation's action, they were involved in the Battle of Frezenberg Ridge. On 8 May, the battalion held the south flank of a dangerous gap in the line against a German assault on their positions on the ridge just north northeast of Bellewaarde Lake. Supported by other British units and some Canadian artillery, the PPCLI managed to hold their position despite losing 392 casualties in one day. The PPCLI soon afterward reverted to Canadian command, becoming part of the new Second Canadian Division when it arrived.

The cost for the Canadian Division in the Second Battle of Ypres had been high. Over 6,000 all ranks had been casualties (dead, wounded or captured). The untested Canadians had taken on a hardened opponent in a novel situation. Despite being eventually beaten back, the Canadian Division had proven that it was a tough nut to crack. It had risen to the challenge of modern warfare and had acquitted itself well. The Division moved into reserve for rest and reinforcement.

Less than two weeks after the gas attacks during the Second Battle of Ypres, the Canadian Division moved south, back into France, to an area east of the village of Festubert. In response to French pressure to attack, the British command decided to move against a small salient in the German lines. Despite the introduction of new British tactics of greater artillery preparatory bombardment and geographically concentrated attacks, the offensive fell short of the mark because of a shortage of ammunition, smaller calibre (and thus less effective) guns than those used by the Germans, poor maps and strong enemy entrenchments. This fighting during the period 15-21 May 1915 was a frustrating experience for the Canadians and everyone else, expensive in lives with little ground gained to show for the effort. Repeated attacks were met with fiercely accurate German artillery and strong machine gun fire. The Canadian casualties during this period were almost 2500 and the German units remained essentially in place.

Things were a little better in June as the division was moved slightly farther south, almost to the bottom end of the larger broad Ypres Salient. The Canadian soldiers were, for a change, on dry high ground with the La Basse Canal anchoring their right flank. The objectives of the Canadian offensive on 15 June were two German trench strong points, H2 and H3, east of the village of Givenchy-lez-la-Bassée to protect the flank of the British 4th Corps attack to the east and north, part of the Artois offensive.

Aerial view of a gas attack. (CWM, 19790555-011)

These attacks, although ultimately unsuccessful, introduced the careful planning and use of artillery that would become a hallmark of Canadian operations throughout the war. Artillery was massed and the guns concentrated upon cutting the wire in front of the enemy positions, afterwards providing a moving barrage to protect the advancing infantry. Three guns were sited to deliver direct fire on to known machine gun positions. A large underground mine was exploded to stun the defenders.

Unfortunately, artillery tactics had not yet progressed to the degree that counter-battery work - deliberate targeting of enemy artillery battery positions - was normal procedure.   The result was that German artillery, always effective, was able to break up advancing Canadian infantry and prepare the way for the inevitable German counterattack.   Wire cutting was effective on some places, in others not so successful. The firing of the mine was short of the target due to technical reasons.   In an attempt to remedy this, the charge of explosive was increased and this resulted in friendly fire casualties. Stubborn German resistance foiled all but minor advances by attacking troops.   Some further attacks were made on 16 June, again to no avail.   The story had been the same in other nearby divisional areas and the Artois offensive was eventually called off across the British front by 19 June.

The Second Battle of Ypres is a well-recognized battle and the monument known as The Brooding Soldier stands in silent vigil at St Julien as testament to the deeds of First Division. But the battles of Festubert and Givenchy today are mostly commemorated only on the regimental colours and guidons of the units that fought in those actions, or on the sides of cenotaphs. There are few markers on the actual ground to remind visitors of the Canadian contribution. Together, the battles of Second Ypres, Festubert and Givenchy had been costly.

Beginning in late June and for the next three months of 1915, the Canadian Division occupied 4400 yards of static trench lines in the Ploegsteert-Messines sector of the Ypres Salient as part of 3rd British Corps. There was little offensive action, relatively speaking, during this period and the interlude provided a time for the Division to rest and refit. Of course, there were the inevitable trenches to construct, re-build and improve and, as always seemed to be the case, time out of battle was filled with physical hard labour.

Out of 11,000 in the division, over 9,000 had been captured, killed or wounded.

*"...And then when it came along towards us it turned green, a
greeny yellow colour. It came up and went over the trenches
and two fellows, one on my right and one on my left, they
dropped and both died."*
Lester Stevens, 8th Battalion
CBC Radio, In Flanders Fields
Episode 5, "THe Second Battle of Ypres"

John McCrae with his dog Bonneau. (NAC, C-046284)

In Flanders fields the poppies blow
Between the crosses, row on row,
That mark our place; and in the sky
The larks, still bravely singing, fly
Scarce heard amid the guns below.

We are the Dead. Short days ago
We lived, felt dawn, saw sunset glow,
Loved, and were loved, and now we lie,
In Flanders fields.

Take up our quarrel with the foe:
To you from failing hands we throw
The torch; be yours to hold it high.
If ye break faith with us who die
We shall not sleep, though poppies grow
In Flanders fields.

John McCrae.

Poppies grow naturally in disturbed areas and the Western Front was fertile ground. Even today, wild poppies grow abundantly in Flanders. On the northern outskirts of Ypres, tucked into a small space between the main road and the Yser Canal, a Canadian medical unit received casualties from the 1915 battle. It was here at Essex Farm that a medical officer, then-Major John McCrae wrote the famous poem, *In Flanders Fields*. Beside a large bronze plaque at the northern edge of the cemetery are a number of reconstructed dugouts in the side of the canal bank. The man-made caverns are reminiscent of the conditions in which the medical unit carried out its duties to the rear of the front line that was just across the canal to the east. There is now a Commonwealth War Graves Commission Cemetery in that location (left, below).

K.K. Forbes, "Defence of Sanctuary Wood" (CWM, 19880266-001)

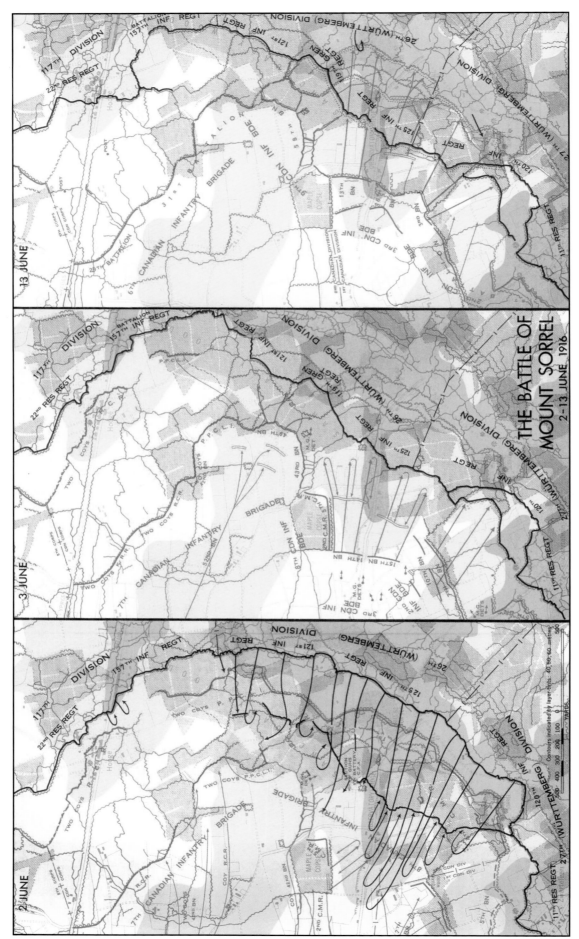

THE BATTLE OF
MOUNT SORREL
2–13 JUNE, 1916

(Courtesy DND Directorate of History and Heritage)

Sir William Newzam Prior Nicholson,
"Canadian Headquarters Staff"
(CWM 19710261-0537).

Photo (right): posing for the painter.
(CWM, CEF Album 7, M440.

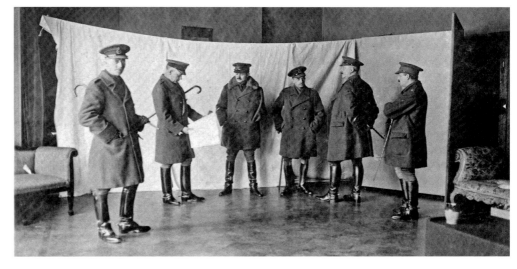

In September 1915, the Canadian Corps was born. The Second Canadian Division had been raised in Canada, dispatched and trained in England and was now moved to France. It was commanded by Major General R.E.W. Turner, a Canadian officer who had won the Victoria Cross in South Africa in 1900.

The division that had already been in action was re-christened First Canadian Division and it was decided that the two Canadian divisions would form the Canadian Corps, much as the Australian and New Zealand troops had formed the ANZAC Corps. British General Alderson became the Corps commander while Canadian Brigadier Arthur Currie was promoted to Major General to command the First Division in Alderson's stead.

ZILLEBEKE

The Village of Zillebeke suffered the same fate as many others in the Ypres Salient - obliteration.   (CWM, CEF Album 6, 4684)

The initial Canadian Corps positions near Ploegsteert were across from German formations, again on higher ground. The Corps executed some diversionary action in support of much larger British and French offensives in the south in the Artois and Champagne regions, but generally the Canadians remained in defensive positions.   The interminable defensive digging continued and, so that the troops would not lose their edge, a routine of trench raids and active patrolling was instituted. Despite being in a static position, the new Canadian Corps lost 688 killed in a total of 2692 casualties between September and December 1915.

The year ended with Third Division being formed and added to the Corps in December. The first two Canadian Corps commanders, Alderson and later Sir Julian Byng, were senior British officers. Throughout the Corps, there were British staff officers at various levels down to brigade headquarters. The small Canadian pre-war army did not have the depth of experience or training to expand as rapidly as events transpired. Few Canadians early in the war had the necessary qualifications and experience in the handling of large army formations.

But as Canadian officers began quickly to gain experience under fire, Canadian authorities began to make strong representations to the British War Office. This resulted, gradually, in a greater number of senior command and staff positions in the Corps being filled by Canadian officers, despite some evident hesitation on the part of the British to relinquish control of Empire troops. Over the next year or two, progressively almost all of the senior positions in the Canadian Corps were to be filled by Canadians. The Canadian Corps was beginning to become a national army.

In early 1916, the three-division Canadian Corps now formed the bulk of the 50,000 troops the Dominion had in the field in Flanders. The Corps was part of Second British Army and deployed in the south part of the Ypres Salient, manning a front of about six miles between Kemmel and Ploegsteert. Poor weather made survival in the trenches a chore in itself. But Army and Corps commanders had their own ideas of how to keep the troops in the line occupied.

Zillebeke today, a modern and typically clean Belgian village.

The Canadian Corps, like other British formations, conducted an offensive defence of their sector. While they had their share of German local attacks and shelling to contend with, the Canadians mounted trench raids to harass the German defenders and to collect information about enemy positions and units. The Canadian Corps seemed to take particularly well to raiding and these operations grew into larger and larger attacks until eventually, by the time of Vimy Ridge in 1917, entire battalions or brigades engaged in these limited operations. The Corps earned a reputation for their efforts during the period January to March 1916. Field Marshal Haig commended them for their aggressiveness. Seigfried Sassoon, the British war poet, in his *Memoirs of an Infantry Officer* almost grudgingly refers to trench raids by "some Canadian toughs", with the clear implication that this was setting a standard, perhaps one not to be envied if one's own battalion was called upon to emulate it.

YSER CANAL

(CWM, CEF Album 6, 4682))

The Yser Canal (above) was used for the transport of cloth and other goods to Ypres in medieval times. This is one of many canals and drainage ditches that are found in this part of Belgium. The banks became logical places for troops to defend or dig in for protection. On the far bank one can discern dug-outs and an observation post up a tree. Medical units were on the near bank and a bridge can be seen down the canal.

Today the Yser Canal is used mainly by light barges and pleasure craft. The canal ends in a yacht basin (photo below right) on the outskirts of Ypres, no longer going all the way to the Cloth Hall. Along the banks, groomed trails take the place of tow paths. Picnic areas and medieval fortifications draw tourists.

To the right of the cyclist above is the path leading to the Essex Farm Commonwealth War Graves Commission Cemetery where there are preserved dug-outs used by medical units in the Great War. The German lines were across the canal and sometimes as close as a few kilometres away. Casualties were brought here from the Second Battle of Ypres, often Canadians who had been caught in the gas attacks of April 1915.

Mines that were blown left the ground transformed. One of the few remaining craters is that at Spanbroekmolen, 7 kilometres south of Ypres, preserved as a memorial and called "The Pool of Peace". (CWM, CEF Album 6, 4681)

A major and frustrating event unfolded for the Second Canadian Division in the early part of April 1916. On 27 March, British engineers blew six massive underground mines in the St Eloi area. German and British troops both were shocked at the size of the explosions and the destruction caused. The explosions created a lunar landscape and the attacking British troops mistakenly seized the wrong objectives. None the wiser, these positions were handed over to Canadian troops on 4 April.

The size of the positions, the lack of reference points in the new landscape and misinformation given by the troops who followed up the explosions perpetuated the errors. German counterattacks, lack of communication, poor map and air photo reading, and lack of adequate artillery support were too much for the Second Division. Patrols and occupying Canadian units became disoriented and suffered badly under continual German shelling. For two weeks the Canadians held on to whatever they could in confused fighting over the often wet ground. Eventually, the mistakes were sorted and the front was consolidated where it stood by mid-month.

The St Eloi Craters cost the Second Division dearly. Its units had sustained almost 1400 casualties. In the quest for reasons for the debacle, a number of British officers at the battalion, brigade, divisional and army level were immediately relieved or re-assigned.

In the Canadian Corps, General Alderson commented adversely upon one brigade commander and upon the performance of General Turner, the divisional commander. Senior British officers realized that a serious situation was developing in British-Canadian relations as a result of ill feeling caused by the fiasco. Some Canadians felt that their own commanders were being made scapegoats for the errors of British units during the action. In the event, General Alderson was the one to move in the following month to become the Inspector General of Canadian Forces in England.

In June of 1916, with the concurrence of the Canadian Government, Field Marshall General Sir Douglas Haig (the Commander in Chief of the British Expeditionary Force) appointed a new commander of the Canadian Corps, Lieutenant General Sir Julian Byng (a British former cavalry officer). Second Division was still manning positions in the St Eloi area while First and Third Divisions were strung out to the left manning the most eastward part of the Ypres Salient. From the village of Hooge in the north, south past Hill 62 (named for the map marking of its height above sea level), the Canadian lines guarded an important part of the arc in the Allied line. The Third Division positions on the left were particularly vital.

"We knew it was going to be a cushy trip because we'd got raspberry jam instead of apricot jam and everything was lovely in the garden. And then, bingo, the next morning all hell broke loose, and there was no let-up."
J.H. Lee, PPCLI
CBC Radio, In Flanders Fields
Episode 7, "Apprentices at Arms"

Sanctuary Wood Cemetery with the actual Sanctuary Wood in the background. The Hill 62 Memorial Garden is beyond the wood .

Canadian trenches after the attack in June 1916 at the battle at Hill 62. (CWM, CEF Album 1, 0158)

A visit to the present-day memorial garden at Hill 62 shows why (see photos next page). It commemorates that major action known variously as the Battle of Sanctuary Wood or the Battle of Mount Sorrel from 2 to 13 June 1916. On the present day road from Ypres to Menin, just short of the village of Hooge, a country lane lined with maple trees veers off to the southeast. On the south side of "Canadalaan", one comes across Sanctuary Wood Cemetery and, a little farther along, a private museum dedicated to the battle. Continuing to the end of the lane, there is a Canadian memorial garden. The woods to the right rear of the garden steps are Sanctuary Wood, so named previously by the British as a place of relative rest for troops not in the immediate front line.

The memorial garden gives an excellent view of the village of Hooge to the north and rolling, partly wooded terrain to the south. All these areas were localities occupied by Third Canadian Division. The memorial garden here is in roughly the position that was occupied by the PPCLI battalion, now part of the Third Division. From it, one has a distant view of the city of Ypres to the northwest, the reason why these heights were so important. From this area, artillery observers could detect movement into and out of the city. The high ground was key terrain. This was one of the few parts of the ridges surrounding Ypres not occupied by the Germans, and they desperately wanted to take it over.

Then and now views along "Canadalaan", the laneway leading to Sanctuary Wood and Hill 62.

On the morning of 2 June 1916, one of the most violent German artillery barrages to that point in the war struck the Canadian lines. Parts of trenches, and the soldiers manning them, were obliterated. The positions held by 4th Canadian Mounted Rifles, a cavalry unit acting as infantry, took the brunt of the German offensive in their position near Armagh Wood. A full 89 percent of the unit became casualties. Also killed in the bombardment was the Third Division commander, who was visiting the forward positions when the full fury fell. With command and control in turmoil and shellfire continuing, the Canadians tried to hold on. As the battle progressed, beneath them German engineers detonated four mines. German infantry then attacked with another fearsome weapon, flame throwers.

Looking back on Ypres from Hill 62 (above), one can see why the Germans wanted to occupy this high ground. After 1914 the vegetation would have been substantially eliminated, along with most of the intervening buildings. If actual targets could not be seen, dust from moving columns of troops or steam from trains arriving and departing would give something at which to shoot..

Some idea of the damage caused by continual artillery bombardment can be seen in the lower pictures. The road shown is the one leading from the Lille Gate to the Cloth Hall in Ypres, then and now. (CWM, CEF Album 1, 0466)

It was all too much and the Canadian line slipped back about 600 yards before reserve units could mount an effective defence line in the evening. In fact it was only an uncharacteristic lack of initiative by the Germans as they stopped to consolidate their gains that saved the day from being a complete rout. Hasty Canadian counterattacks on the morning of 3 June were poorly coordinated and succeeded only in closing some of the gaps in the line.

After a short period of defensive construction by both sides, including the seizure of part of the Hooge positions by the Germans, the Canadian Corps was reinforced with artillery and set about to give the Germans a taste of their own mdeicine with heavy concentrations of shellfire. Poor weather hampered registration of the guns. Preparations for the Somme farther south on the British front precluded much reinforcement of the Corps. However, General Byng set 13 June as the date for a Corps counteroffensive to re-capture the southernmost German gains that had put them only two miles from Ypres.

The First Division conducted the main attack, beginning in the early morning hours in rain and under cover of smoke, supported by Second Division on their northern flank. Massive artillery bombardments during the preceding week kept the Germans on edge and did to them what they had done to the Canadians. Smashed by overwhelming firepower, the defenders had little chance to resist. The Canadian attack, the first planned and executed as a deliberate Corps operation by its own headquarters, was a success in only a matter of hours.

The Canadian units had suffered an initial defeat. No amount of rationalization could erase that fact. However, under the leadership of Byng

and employing proper co-ordination and tactics, the Canadians regained the lost ground and in the process moved a quantum step forward in their own professionalism.

The following month was spent in the Salient, manning the trenches and rotating to rear areas for rest and training. Trench lines were straightened and strengthened. King George V visited the Corps Headquarters and minor operations, including raids and seizing craters blown by British and German engineers, and various infantry battalions and artillery units in turn took the battle to the enemy.

The time in the Ypres Salient had been a steep learning curve for the Canadians. The Canadian Corps had grown quickly in size and experience. In a little over a year, in addition to learning the intricacies of trench warfare, they had acquitted themselves well in a major battle that heralded a new dimension in warfare, poison gas. In more minor operations, they had proven to be hard fighters, perhaps not always successfully but always with tenacity. In the first major deliberate attack operation of the formation, the Canadian Corps regained the ground lost previously at Hill 62 with resiliency and elan. Both enemy and allied commanders began to note the robust, aggressive action that was becoming characteristic of the Canadian Corps units.

By the end of July 1916, the Canadian Corps was set to move to a new battlefield, the Somme, to join one of the most violent and wasteful battles ever to be fought on the Western Front.

Royal visit by King George V. (CWM, CEF Album 1, 0639)

"There was no trenches left when we got there. The men were being rushed in in column of fours and it was just like pouring metal into a blast furnace. They just dissolved as they got in under the curtain of fire. They just seemed to dissolve."
S.R. Bowe, 2nd Canadian Mounted Rifles
CBC Radio, In Flanders Fields
Episode 7, "Apprentices at Arms"

Upham

Bombardment
Fricourt June 30

W.T. Topham, "Somme Bombardment in Full Swing" (CWM, 1971026I-0725)

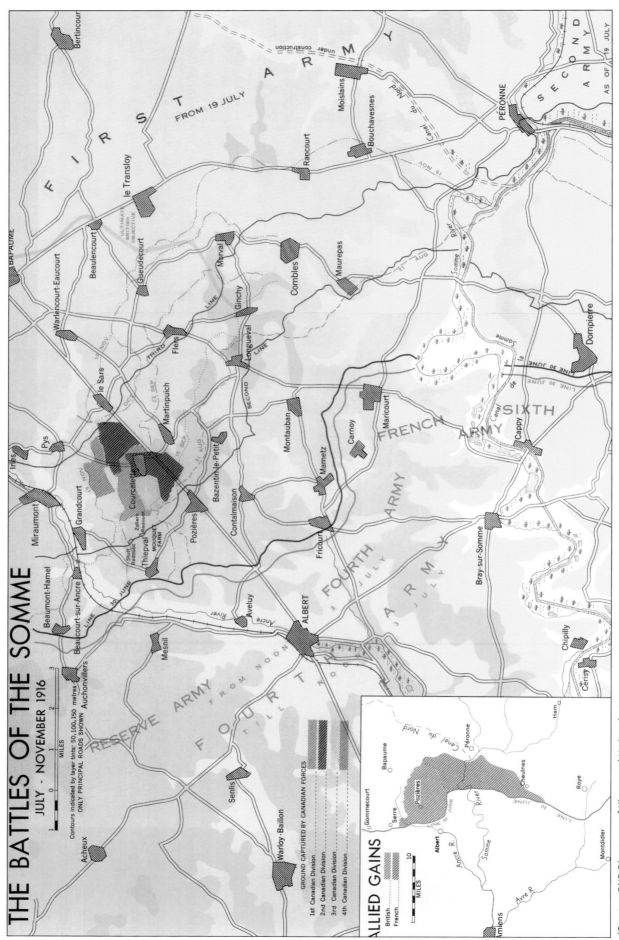

THE BATTLES OF THE SOMME

JULY - NOVEMBER 1916

MILES

Contours indicated by layer tints: 50,100,150 metres
ONLY PRINCIPAL ROADS SHOWN

GROUND CAPTURED BY CANADIAN FORCES

1st Canadian Division
2nd Canadian Division
3rd Canadian Division
4th Canadian Division

FIRST ARMY

FROM 19 JULY

SECOND ARMY

AS OF 19 JULY

Bertincourt
Bapaume
Warlencourt-Eaucourt
Beaulencourt
le Transloy
Gueudecourt
ULTIMATE BRITISH OBJECTIVE
Flers
Martinpuich
le Sars
22 SEP
15 SEP
27 AUG
Courcelette
Pys
Irles
Miraumont
Grandcourt
Zollern Redoubt
Sturt Redoubt
Thiepval
MOUQUET FARM
Pozières
Bazentin-le-Petit
Contalmaison
Beaumont-Hamel
Beaucourt-sur-Ancre
LINE 30 JUNE
Mesnil
Auchonvillers
Acheux
RESERVE ARMY
Senlis
Warloy-Baillon
Aveluy
Ancre River
ALBERT
FROM NOON TILL NOON
FOURTH ARMY
3 JULY
Fricourt
Mametz
Montauban
Carnoy
Maricourt
Longueval
Ginchy
Combles
Morval
Rancourt
Moislains
Bouchavesnes
PÉRONNE
LINE 19 NOV
Maurepas
FRENCH ARMY
SIXTH ARMY
Cappy
Bray-sur-Somme
Chipilly
Cerisy
31 AUG
Somme River
Canal du Nord
under construction
LINE 30 JUNE
Dompierre
THIRD LINE
SECOND LINE
NOV

ALLIED GAINS

British
French
MILES   10

Gommecourt
Serre
Bapaume
Péronne
Ham
Pozières
Albert
Ancre R.
Somme River
LINE 30 JUNE
Chaulnes
Roye
Montdidier
Avre R.
Amiens
Canal du Nord

48

(Courtesy DND Directorate of History and Heritage)

A Canadian photographic crew (above) takes pictures to record the achievements of the Canadian Corps on the battlefield. Cumbersome equipment and the dangers of the front line meant that film in particular often resulted in long-range and indistinct products. To overcome this, battle scenes were sometimes staged to depict the war to an audience. (CWM, CEF Album 1, 0851)

There is nothing staged about the picture below, however. A shellburst is caught in mid-explosion outside the town of Courcelette , one of the Canadian objectives. (CWM, CEF Album 1, 0852)

BEAUMONT HAMEL

Although not part of the Canadian Corps at the time, because its members hailed from a separate self-governing colony, The Royal Newfoundland Regiment took part in the initial actions on the Somme, 1 July 1916. The unit was part of the British 29th Division and, near the village of Beaumont Hamel, attacked well-entrenched German positions as part of the general offensive. The results were disastrous, and from the one battalion casualties quickly mounted to almost 700 men in an hour's fighting. It was later said that there was almost no village or outport in Newfoundland that was not touched by the casualty list. In contrast to the present day Canada Day celebrations elsewhere, the First of July still holds a sombre tinge of remembrance in Newfoundland to this day.

A huge statue of a caribou, the insignia of the unit, is found surmounting an old bunker at the battlefield park at Beaumont Hamel, and at other locations in France and Belgium where Newfoundlanders fought. In the park are the names of men of the island colony who were listed as missing during the war. The complete story of the Newfoundlanders at Beaumont Hamel is commemorated and told by interpreters at the Canadian government-operated battlefield park. Some of the best-preserved examples of original trench systems and shell holes on the Western Front can be seen here from the top of the monument.

The sadness of Beaumont Hamel was assuaged somewhat in October when the Newfoundlanders attacked and occupied German positions in the area of the village of Gueudecourt, just a few kilometres south of Bapaume and east of Courcelette. As part of the British 12th Division, the battalion captured and successfully defended Hilt Trench from determined counterattacks over a period of two and a half days. Another caribou now stands guard over the site of the 239 casualties, including 120 killed.

A.Y. Jackson, "Vimy Ridge from Souchez Valley" (CWM, 19710261-0171)

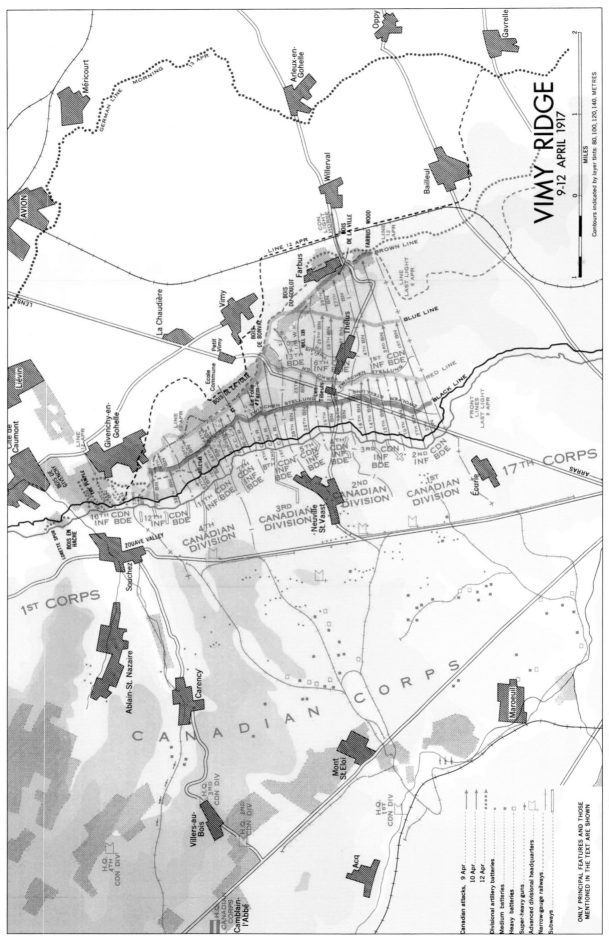

VIMY RIDGE
9-12 APRIL 1917

Contours indicated by layer tints: 80, 100, 120, 140, METRES

MILES

Canadian attacks, 9 Apr
10 Apr
12 Apr
Divisional artillery batteries
Medium batteries
Heavy batteries
Super-heavy guns
Advanced divisional headquarters
Narrow-gauge railways
Subways

ONLY PRINCIPAL FEATURES AND THOSE
MENTIONED IN THE TEXT ARE SHOWN

(Courtesy DND Directorate of History and Heritage)

VIMY RIDGE & HILL 70

After the Somme, the Canadian Corps moved to the area north of Arras and held a ten-mile front for the last few weeks of 1916 and the first three months of 1917. Eventually, the Fourth Canadian Division joined the Corps after it was released from British command on the Somme. The interval was marked by periodic trench routine punctuated by artillery duels, routine rotation of units into and out of the front line, aggressive patrolling and trench raids. In this period the Germans, too, were busy improving their defences in the area. They were experimenting with a more elastic defensive posture, better able to absorb the punishing shell-fire and subsequent infantry attacks that were now characteristics of the Allied offensives. The task given to the Canadian Corps in the spring of 1917 was a big one - to assault Vimy Ridge, a major feature that dominated the low ground to the west and provided observation for the enemy all the way to Arras. This operation was really subsidiary to larger concurrent British and French offensives on the flanks, but it has become a defining moment in Canadian history.

The 29th Battalion (above) moves up to take part in the assault in one of the successive phases of the battle of Vimy Ridge. Part of the 6th Canadian Infantry Brigade, the battalion went into the assault at about 0930 hrs after the 4th Brigade had cleared enemy elements up to the Red Line, the first phase task of the Second Division. The second phase operation went precisely as planned and as practiced. The 29th Battalion moved into action through the shelled village of Thélus and seized the high ground beyond. Note the limited visibility on the morning of 9 April and the Lewis machine gun on the shoulder of the man in the centre. One assumes that the battalion is not yet in action because of the casual way that the men are holding their weapons. The effect of the artillery bombardments is clearly visible on the chewed-up ground. Wire obstacles appear to have been cleared from the stakes at the left.

CWM, CEF Album 2, 1162)

"We were an entirely different army than at the Somme, and I suppose that some of the terrible things that happened at the Somme were of some benefit in turning out the type of army that we had at Vimy."
E.S. Russenholt, 44th Battalion
CBC Radio, In Flanders Fields
Episode 9, "The Battle of Vimy Ridge"

(Below) The western slopes of the ridge up which the Canadians attacked on Easter Monday, 9 April 1917, were not as wooded then as they are now. They were bare and pocked with shell holes and trench lines, dugouts and concrete machine gun bunkers. Many shell holes, now grassed over and less sharply defined, are still evident along the road that leads to the top of the hill. A reconstructed trench line and craters from previous battles are near the Grange Tunnel system and open for tourists to walk through. Sheep, visible in the contemporary photo below, keep the grass trimmed, blissfully unaware of the still-dangerous ordinance hidden just below the grass.

"The artillery did everything it said it would do, and I could hardly put my hand on the ground w ithout seeing where shrapnel had gone in."
T.G. Caunt, 8th Battalion
CBC Radio, In Flanders Fields
Episode 9, "The Battle of Vimy Ridge"

Allied forces had tried earlier, in vain, to capture the ridge. Now it was the turn of General Byng and the Canadian Corps. For the first time, all four Canadian divisions would be used together on the battlefield. Soldiers from all parts of the country mingled and fought together, and won a major victory that put the Canadian war effort into sharp perspective among other Allied efforts. For that combination of battlefield success and national identity, Vimy Ridge occupies a seminal position in the Canadian psyche.

The Canadians had had time to absorb the lessons of their earlier experiences in the Ypres Salient and in the Somme. Additionally, Major General Currie, the First Division commander, had been given the chance to observe and report upon French operations. Byng and the Corps staff now put into practice the distilled ideas. In their view, a number of factors were vital: planning and preparation, co-ordination of artillery support with infantry movement, limited objectives in time and space, and quick reinforcement to consolidate new defensive positions against counterattack. The Canadian Corps scheme of operations issued on 5 March 1917 for the forthcoming assault took all of this into account.

Realistic objectives were broken into attainable phases not too far distant and apportioned to battalions in turn. Artillery fire plans commenced with a heavy preliminary bombardment on enemy infantry, artillery and rear area positions well ahead of time to neutralize and harass German units. A strict artillery timetable was devised for each phase of the Canadian attack and infantry units were trained to keep close to their own barrage, to "lean into the artillery". Follow-up units were designated to mop up by-passed enemy bunkers and strong points and to handle prisoners and casualties. Machine gun detachments were to move forward quickly to consolidate positions after capture. Most importantly, units studied and rehearsed their roles in the larger picture. Replicas of observed German positions were outlined in marker tape laid over ground in rear areas. Units walked through their designated assault objectives while officers simulated artillery fire and pointed out known enemy strong points. Maps were issued to the lowest levels of command.

*Wounded moving back on light tramway from Vimy Ridge.
(CWM, CEF Album 1, 0812)*

Incredibly, all these preparations had to be undertaken under the direct observation of the enemy on the ridge. Consequently, much of the work was restricted to hours of darkness. But much of the preparation was done underground. Engineers dug tunnels and improved existing subterranean paths to provide thirteen covered assembly areas and routes. Some pre-existing chalk caves were used, some from medieval mine works and others constructed by army tunnelling companies. In some cases the chambers were big enough to hold a complete battalion together. The tunnel works still exist and trained guides lead visitors today through the Grange Tunnel at Vimy Memorial battlefield park.

Combat units were not the only ones kept busy. Light gauge railways (below) were laid close to the front to allow ammunition and supply dumps to grow by over 800 tons per day. Railway troops also assembled tramways so that they could be pushed forward immediately after objectives were captured. About 300 carts were designated for the evacuation of the wounded alone (photo above). Water points had to be constructed and over 45 miles of pipeline was laid to provide 600,000 gallons of water daily for the men and the over 50,000 horses and mules.

(CWM, CEF Album 2, 2106)

In 1922, the French government gave the area of the summit of the ridge to the Canadian government for a memorial park. The visitor to the massive Vimy Memorial, designed and constructed by Walter Allward over a period of ten years, sits astride the highest point of the ridge, Hill 145. It is the largest of all the Canadian Great War European monuments and certainly one of the most impressive on the continent, dominating as it does the vista for over 60 kilometres in every direction. The construction and unveiling of "le Mémorial", as the French refer to it, is a story in itself. However, the casual visitor can be easily misled by the scope of the event that even such a large memorial commemorates.

If one had been in the area of the monument during the attack, only about two of the assaulting battalions would have been visible. Another 17 battalions of all four divisions in the Canadian Corps moved from west to east in line abreast, stretching south of Hill 145 to the Arras-Lens road. To the north, another two battalions advanced in the same way. Under a snow and sleet storm, 983 guns of all calibres fired together at 5:30 a.m. on 9 April, obliterating parts of German trenches, command bunkers and artillery positions. Infantry moved out of their assembly areas, through the tunnels and into the open. They closed up to the protective barrages and advanced with their carefully timed and practised rate of advance of one hundred yards each three minutes - the "Vimy glide", as it was described by one pilot flying overhead.

Vimy Memorial from the Douai Plain. (Pepper Mintz)

All the preparations paid off. Enemy troops were caught in their bunkers. Those that resisted were overcome either by leading or follow-up units designated to collect prisoners and eliminate by-passed pockets. At the first phase line, the Black Line, the lead Canadians paused for a planned interval and then follow-on units moved forward to resume the attack with artillery support. This was repeated at the Red Line, reached by the troops of the First and Second Divisions by 8:00 a.m. The same clockwork sequence was repeated for the Blue Line. Eventually the First and Second Divisions reached the final Brown Line by last light of 9 April after they had swept up opposition in and around the village of Thélus and to the south.

Strong resistance caused the fighting on the top of the ridge to go on all day and into the next. Third and Fourth Division soldiers eventually cleared Hill 145 and surrounding eastern slopes to the extent of their initial objective areas by the afternoon of 10 April. This part of the battle was hard fought and required extra reserves to be inserted into the fray to finally overcome the enemy.

Still remaining to be captured was a feature north of Hill 145 called The Pimple. This was a hill just east of the village of Souchez. When smoke and snow abated, enemy machine guns and artillery observers on The Pimple could fire upon Hill 145. Troops initially intended for this objective had earlier been used on Hill 145, so a rest of 48 hours was called and then 10th Brigade of Fourth Division attacked it on 12 April at 5:00 a.m., again in snow and mud, under a thunderous barrage of over 100 guns. By daybreak that morning, The Pimple was in Canadian hands. Subsequent operations in the south extended the Canadian lines to include the wooded areas at the northeastern foot of the ridge and as far east as the village of Farbus and the Lens-Arras railway line.

The Battle of Vimy Ridge was hailed as a great victory by the Allied press and recounted as a great loss for the Germans. Over a front of 7,000 yards, the Canadian Corps had advanced for about 4,500 yards, seizing guns, mortars, trenches and machine guns along with 4,000 prisoners. Most importantly, as anyone visiting the monument can plainly see, the ridge afforded a view of the Douai Plain to the east and the approaches to the city of Lens, a major mining and industrial centre. Now exposed to Allied artillery observers, the German army had to move its troops about four miles east to new, less visible, positions. In some of the withdrawals, further enemy losses were inflicted. As for the Canadian Corps, the six-day battle had cost 10,602 casualties, among them almost 3,600 killed.

After Vimy Ridge, the Canadians and the Allies adjusted their fronts. During the late part of April and into May-June, Canadian formations made limited attacks to clear enemy positions in the Arleux and Fresnoy areas east of Vimy Ridge. Two Canadian brigades also conducted a massive raid in the Souchez-Avion sector. This latter, a complicated and successful foray, was a mark of the sophisticated level of staff planning, co-ordination and execution that the Canadian Corps had attained in its approach to warfare. All these operations were part of an active defence program that culminated in a general advance along the front.

Artillery ammunition is being opened from crates and placed into horse-drawn field artillery limbers for immediate use in action. Vimy Ridge is visible in the background (above). The limber carriages held equipment and stores for the gun crew and the horses drawing it. (CWM, CEF Album 2, 1437)

It was common practice (below) to dump ammunition in the open for short periods so that units could pick it up within a reasonable distance from their positions, or enroute to new positions. Dumping ammunition also freed up transport units to do other tasks and not have to await the arrival of the destination unit. Breaking down ammunition from its transport packaging is time-consuming and called for maximum effort from all members of an artillery unit. Crates and packing material would be salvaged for re-use. There would have been little threat of enemy shelling at this time since the German forces were well to the north and northeast after the Canadian victory in seizing the ridge. In any event, the unit would be out of observation range of enemy guns. (CWM, CEF Album 3, 2104)

BOSQUET CHIMNEYS OF FOSSE 6 J36A FOSSE 3 & 15 SALLAUMINES HIGHGROUND IN K17 BRIDGE N35c88 RAILWAY EMBANKMENT MONTIGNY Ch. MONS-EN-PEVELE CITÉ BOISGELIN FOSSE 2 HOUSE N35c2·1 BOIS DE L'OFFL FOS

64 65 66 67

(CWM 19810052-026)

AT FOSSE 2 BILLY MONT CHURCH Y RAILWAY

MERICOURT

BIS

68

Artillery observers (above) man an Observation Post (OP) looking towards Arleux after consolidation on and forward of Vimy Ridge. Subsequent to the battle, Canadians pushed out their line to follow up the withdrawing German forces who were forced from their positions by the loss of the ridge. Here a small group of the Forward Observation Officer and his assistants use a telescope to spot the fire of guns farther back. They would be in communication with the gun positions by field telephone. (CWM, CEF Album 2, 1315)

Canadian artillery was very effective by the time of Vimy Ridge. The fire of British and Canadian guns was centrally controlled at very high level, in contrast to the German army that tended to apportion fire units to much junior formations. Consequently, Allied artillery could be switched and concentrated quickly in much higher volumes to meet specific needs of the troops. While front-line commanders always wanted more fire support, many war diaries commented favourably upon the artillery effectiveness in various operations.

Military mapping reached new levels of quality on the Western Front. Both sides had extensive geographic engineer survey units and printed constantly-updated maps containing great detail. Trench maps were often done in scales of 1:10,000 (that is, a very detailed, large scale map). In addition, specialized artillery survey confirmed the location of all gun positions so that accurate firing calculations could be done. Other survey units were organized to detect the location of enemy guns and Canadian artillery offiicers played a major role in this type of counter-battery work, using sound ranging and flash spotting to pinpoint gun positions that were later silenced by pre-planned artillery barrages during both defensive and offensive operations.

The picture above left is an extract from a larger panoramic photo used by artillery observers as a range card. On the photo are marked prominent landmarks and the map or compass bearings from a particular OP to them. The photographic range card would be passed from observer to observer as they were relieved in place. Each observer would constantly improve the range data as it became available. Targets or obvious positions would be similarly marked on maps at the gun position and the information would be disseminated to all artillery units in range in the form of target lists. It would then be a simple matter for an observer to call down fire or make clear reference to specific places on his front.

The panorama extract is from a photo taken in 1917 looking toward Lens from Hill 145 on Vimy Ridge, the location of the Canadian Memorial today. The lower picture is from the same position.

FARBUS

(CWM, CEF Album 2, 0112)

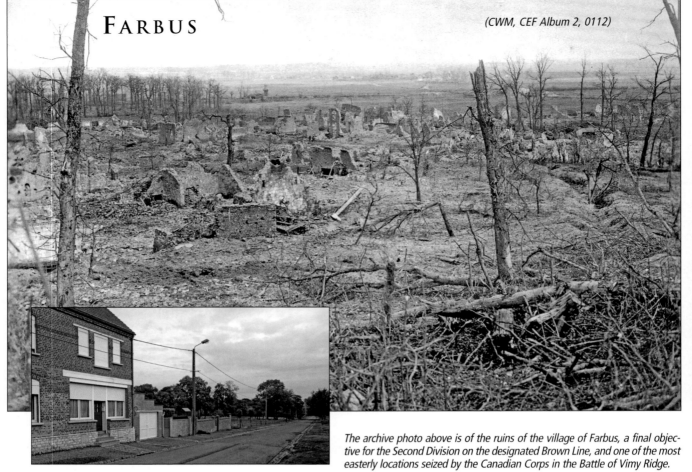

The archive photo above is of the ruins of the village of Farbus, a final objective for the Second Division on the designated Brown Line, and one of the most easterly locations seized by the Canadian Corps in the Battle of Vimy Ridge.

The village barely discernable in the distance is Willerval. After the village was taken, infantry patrols pushed out to a railway line between the two localities and a cavalry patrol of the Canadian Light Horse went to the far village and returned. Farbus was one of the farthest enemy objectives from the Start Line of the attack and artillery support was starting to wear thin because of the distance. In accordance with a previously timed plan, the First and Second Divisions paused long enough to bring forward machine guns and to allow artillery units within range to shift their fire to better distribute it along the front.

(Below) Artillery firing at night. (CWM, CEF Album 2, 1321)

(Left) The ruined church at Ablain St Nazaire near Vimy Ridge struck a special chord with the local citizens who preserved it as a memorial to the Great War.

(Top) The summit of the hill in the background of the archival photograph is the site of the present day French war memoiral and cemetery, Notre Dame de Lorette (see Chapter 11). (CWM, CEF Album 3, 2510)

(Centre) The scene resonated also with Canadian war artists, several of whom treated it as a subject. This rendition is by John William Beatty. (CWM, 19710261-0100)

Currie and staff, Ypres (CWM, CEF Album 3, 2235)

In June 1917, Canadian Lieutenant General Arthur Currie replaced British Lieutenant General Julian Byng as the Canadian Corps commander. One month later, the Canadian Corps was ordered to prepare for another difficult battle: the Battle for Hill 70. In fact, this battle is less well known than Vimy Ridge but it may have been just as momentous. It was the first battle the Canadian Corps fought under completely Canadian command with General Currie at the helm. As well, the battle had the important tactical aim of threatening the Germans with an advance on the British front towards Lille.

In July of 1917, the Canadian Corps moved to its left, away from the Vimy Ridge area overlooking the Douai Plain east of the ridge, and into positions formerly occupied by 1st British Corps north of Souchez. The Corps' divisions stretched to a point a mile east of Loos. The units of the Corps continued to mount raids and patrol along the front.

Currie's orders in early July were to capture the city of Lens. In considering the problem, Currie realized that, even if his attack was successful, the city itself would not be tenable if the high ground at Hill 70 north of the city was not taken. However, occupying Hill 70 would make life unbearable for the German units in the lower ground. By seizing the feature, Currie reasoned, his formation could quickly establish a strong defensive position and use its artillery and infantry strength as an anvil upon which the Germans could be smashed when they counterattacked, as they surely would. Currie therefore argued with his superiors for a change in his operational objective, something that must have been no small feat for a brand-new corps commander. He was persuasive, and planning began accordingly.

Bad weather postponed operations until early on the morning of 15 August. Under the cover of a smoke screen and a well-planned artillery program of high explosive and gas shells on both forward and in-depth enemy positions, the Canadian Corps moved eastward with two divisions.

The First and Second Divisions attacked the Hill 70 area from west to east while the Fourth Division at the southern end of the Canadian line mounted subsidiary and diversionary attacks against the outskirts of Lens. Again, the attack was controlled by pre-planned coloured phase lines on maps. Despite some hard fighting in places, most of the objectives were met and strong infantry and machine gun posts were established by nightfall on the first day along the crest. Artillery moved forward to fire with deadly effect upon enemy units assembling for and moving into counterattack positions.

On 17 August, in the face of determined but local and uncoordinated counterattacks by the enemy, the Canadians moved their forward line down the east slope of the Hill 70 feature. The Germans presented the Canadians with the nasty surprise of the first use of mustard gas. Notwithstanding, the Canadian divisions and their coordinated artillery fire presented a sturdy shield of steel upon which German counterattacks shattered. Currie later called the fighting in this period one of the hardest battles of the Canadian Corps. By 18 August, the Canadians were in firm control of most of the Hill 70 area and had beaten back unsuccessful enemy attacks.   Further Canadian operations, some of them only moderately successful, continued until 25 August to clear suburbs of Lens and to remove isolated and minor German salients in the line.

Mine pit heads, Lens.
(CWM, CEF Album 5, 3767)

Canadian soldiers returning from trenches during the Battle of the Somme. Nov. 1916   (NAC, PA-000832)

In the ten days of fighting during 15-25 August, the Canadians suffered almost 9,200 casualties. In return, five German divisions had been severely damaged. This loss posed problems for the German High Command in their apportionment of future reserves along the rest of the Western Front. Allied possession of Hill 70 was a continual threat for the enemy that could not be ignored and was such a strong tactical position that it was never re-captured by the Germans, even during the March 1918 Offensive.

Regrettably, there is no monument to Hill 70. Most of that field of hard battle is now unrecognizable due to urban development. Other than the view of the pitheads and slag heaps of the Lens coalmines readily evident from Vimy Ridge, Hill 70 remains a generally unmarked milestone of Canadian military history.

Red Ensign flown over the Vimy Ridge battlefield.
(On loan from the Imperial War Museum, CWM 20040039-001)

VIMY MEMORIAL

"From Vimy on we were invincible. Nothing could stop us."
Tommy Adams, 85th Battalion
CBC Radio, In Flanders Fields
Epoisode 9, "The Battle of Vimy Ridge"

(Photos: Pepper Mintz)

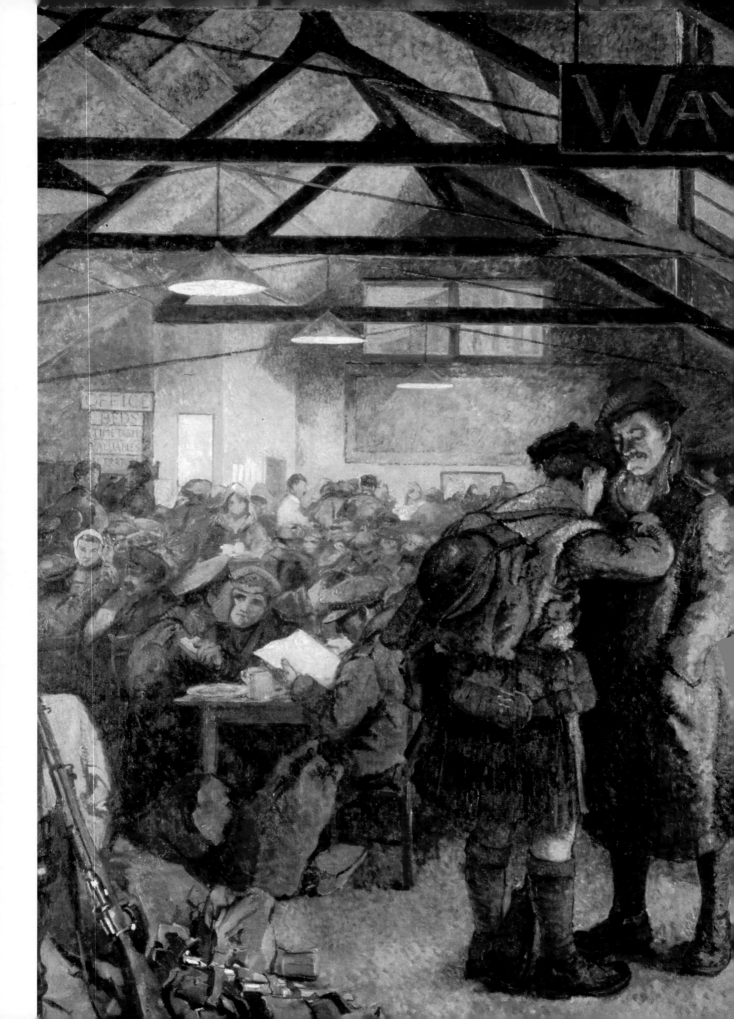

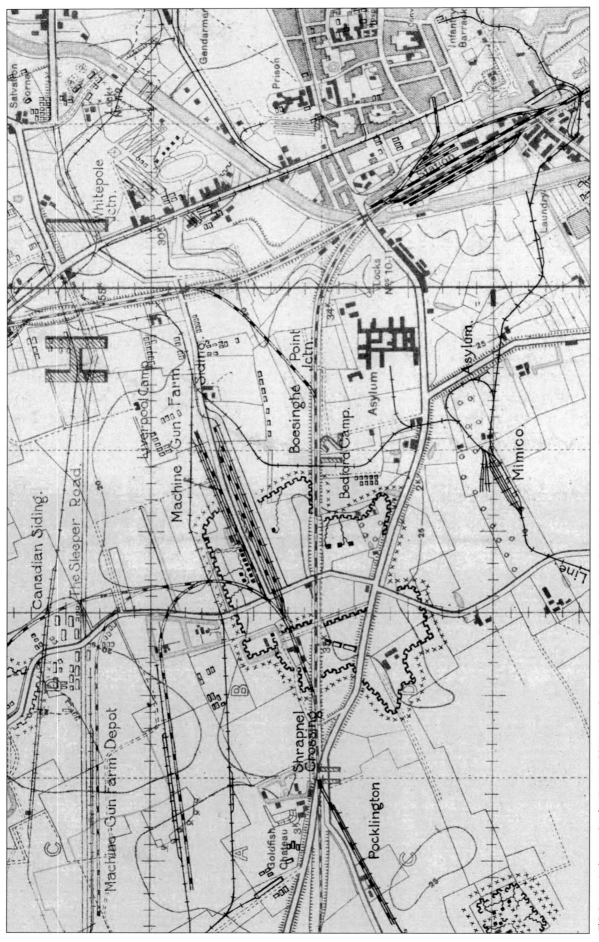

This is a typical example of a First World War trench map. The scale is 1:10,000 and shows a large amount of detail, important for a static war.
This area west of Ypres shows the large number of railway lines laid to supply the troops.
Source: Field Survey Company, Royal Engineers (8534), Map 28NW 4 (Ypres, 1918, Edition 3, trenches corrected to 27.3.18)

THE REAR AREA

Officers and men of the 107th Siege Battery take time out for a group photo somewhere behind the lines. (CWM, CEF Album 1, 0448)

Troops were not always in trenches during the whole war. Indeed, the time actually spent in the very front lines by an individual was normally only a few days of each week that their unit was in the line. The rest of the time was spent in reserve trenches and, even at that, the time was comparatively short. The Canadian Corps followed the British method of constant rotation of units and formations into and out of the line. This was in contrast to the French Army, for instance, that left units in forward positions for extended periods of time.

Not all members of an infantry battalion were employed in the forward trenches. Even in an infantry unit there might be cooks and orderlies and signalers that seldom, if ever, went all the way forward. Similarly, in a brigade or division there were many units that were not normally found in the most exposed trenches abutting the enemy. As one went backwards, the number of supporting troops grew and grew and they occupied real estate in an echelon behind the soldier manning the barbed wire. The infantryman is often likened to the tip of the spear and the others, behind him and supporting him in varying degrees of direct contact, are the shaft and handle.

The Canadian Corps by this time (the summer of 1917) was approximately 100,000 in strength. This organization, about the size in population of a small city today, had all the same day-to-day functions and needs as would any city. While the "industry" of the Canadian Corps was "breaking things and hurting people", there was a constant need to house and feed and clothe the workmen, whether or not they were in holes in the ground or in buildings in rear areas. Huge amounts of supplies, measured in the tons, had to be moved daily from the rear to the front to supply not only the ammunition to be fired but also the daily requirements of individuals, including food. The injured required medical care and fatal casualties had to be collected and buried. Sewage had to be organized and processed. Salvage recycling programs were operated. There had to be a system of law and order, including policing and sanctions for transgressors. Animals had to be fed, tended by veterinarians and replaced. Boots, uniforms, weapons and equipment had to be repaired. Officers and soldiers had to be schooled in their craft, either to refresh themselves on current procedures, or to learn new ideas and innovative equipment as they were introduced and disseminated. Troops had to have places for rest, recreation and recuperation. Meanwhile, those "small cities", the military formations, were expected to be able to move about the battlefield from one sector to another. The rear areas behind the front, and the support systems for the troops, were very sophisticated in their organization.

POPERINGHE

Funeral procession, Poperinghe.. (CWM, CEF Album 3, 2138)

Perhaps one of the best examples of rear area organization was the sector west of the city of Ypres. By 1917, the relatively static Western Front had allowed the British rear area to reach a high level of administrative efficiency. Poperinghe, a pleasant little town today, was known then as "Little Paris" in recognition of its busy streets and the attractions found there by the soldiers on short leave from their units. As a road and rail junction, it was ideal as a staging area for the movement of troops and supplies forward to the trenches east of Ypres. It served as more than that, however. It was a major medical area for the treatment of casualties and, unfortunately, a major burial ground, too. From Poperinghe, wagons and trains fanned out to a myriad of smaller bases between there and the Ypres area. Maps of the day (see trench map detail previous page) show the surrounding area filled with different types of ammunition depots, forward medical units, camps with barracks, remount depots for horses, engineer stores dumps, and bivouac and billet areas for troops not in the line. In the town itself, restaurants, bars, bordellos and various other amusements soon established themselves with willing customers among the troops, many of them semi-permanent residents of the area and others who were visitors sampling the joys of life after having survived another rotation into the front lines. A British military chaplain established Talbot House, or "Toc H" in military message signal parlance, as an informal rest centre. The centre is still there today, affiliated with the In Flanders Field museum, having been replicated globally wherever the British Army served in later years. There were military police units in the town and it holds the grim distinction of being one of the places where a number of executions were carried out after soldiers had been found guilty of desertion or dereliction of duty.

The main square of Poperinghe today.

CANADA CORNER

"Canada Corner", at the junction of present day routes N375 and N315, 10 kilometres southwest of Ypres. In the archival photo (above), the road has been cleared and the presence of the signs indicates that the route would have been a well-travelled one. A staff car with its officer passenger has stopped here, probably to pose this picture.

The car is an indication of the increasing use of motorization by all the armies. Early in the war staff officers actually moved by horseback and on foot when visiting forward units. The automobile allowed better communication between the rear headquarters and troops farther ahead. (CWM, CEF Album 6, 4677)

RENINGHELST

Reninghelst church after bombardment, and beautifully restored today. (CWM, CEF Album 6, 4674)

Reninghelst, four kilometres southeast of Poperinghe, is now an unremarkable village and, being off the main highway, the average tourist would not give it a second glance. It is typical of the small bedroom communities found across the Flanders landscape, its central crossroads dominated by a large church, a few substantial red brick buildings scattered about and farmland on its outskirts. The small cemetery at the church holds a small number of graves from the Second World War. First World War graves are in a larger cemetery on the northwest edge of village.

But in 1917, it was a mini-metropolis. Reflecting Poperinghe, it was called "Little London" by the troops. It was home to about 45,000 Canadian, British, Australian and New Zealand soldiers, and about 15,000 horses. There were many *estaminets* (coffee shops), bivouacs, billets, hospitals, rest areas and reinforcement holding areas. The King even visited Canadians in Reninghelst. One of the most-visited locales was the brick brewery building at Reninghelstplein 6 - a laundry and shower area where the troops went through an assembly line process to bathe and get new or clean uniforms. Troop units coming off the line would be cycled through the establishment.

More than rats and disease, lice was the major complaint of the troops who were living in crowded and dirty conditions. Steaming and boiling of the uniforms did not remove all the flea larvae in the seams. Only in late 1917 did a Canadian medical officer devise a chemical treatment to be used in conjunction with the cleaning process to kill all fleas and their traces.

If one stands beside the road at the side of the church graveyard and looks northeast, one can see a tranquil meadow along the streambed that meanders in the general direction of Ypres (right). In reality, this is the site of a railroad bed, part of a spider web of tracks that ran to the front lines. Tons of ammunition, fodder, food and engineer supplies moved forward and, too often, casualties moved back, all on narrow gauge rails.

(CWM, CEF Album 1, 0813)

The Canadian contribution to railway construction on the Western Front was considerable. In October of 1914, as the Allied war effort was gearing up, the British War Office expressed its need for railway troops. Many Canadians, fresh from the experience of pushing railway lines across the Dominion, wanted to answer the call. The Army Council said that it wanted formed units and not just "labour gangs". Initially, this was not acceptable to the Canadian government. However, in February 1915, Ottawa authorized the provision of 500 railway troops organized into two companies of the new Canadian Overseas Railway Construction Corps. In the first instance, all the soldiers came from the CPR and all had to pass a test of their ability to join. Thus the quality of the railway soldiers was very high. The companies deployed to France by October 1915, after training and movement to Europe, and they were first employed with the Belgians building 60 centimetre tramways. The following month, the companies deployed with Second British Army lines of communication troops in Reningelst.

The existing railheads were 10 to 12 miles (15 to 20 kilometres) from the front. It was here that supplies were transshipped to mainly horse-drawn (but occasionally some motorized) transport for movement to the area immediately behind the trenches and artillery positions. In preparation for the Battle of the Somme, it was decided to begin a program to move the railheads closer, by June 1916 to within three miles of the front. By this time, the tonnages of supplies and ammo that had to be moved were massive. For instance, 1,934 tons of supplies per mile of front were needed daily in the Fourth British Army sector alone.

As it transpired, given the horrible condition of the ground over which the supplies had to be transported, three miles was still not close enough. Therefore, it was decided to install tramways to move supplies even further forward, sometimes right to the rear trenches to replace as many horse-drawn transports, mules or man-pack requirements as possible.

Tramways were narrow gauge tracks that could be laid and repaired quickly. Locomotion was provided either mechanically or by animal or human power.

The Canadian Corps was a leader in this type of tramway building. At Vimy Ridge, tramways were used to move soldiers and supplies forward quickly to prepare for the battle and to reinforce success. Small steel lines were laid right up to the assembly areas of the attack and then, after success, forward into the new positions. Casualties and prisoners were moved quickly backward. In preparation for the Passchendaele operation, Canadian units came to the Ypres salient. Because so much of the area was susceptible to German harassing artillery fire, there were about 100 breaks in the light railway system each day from enemy shellfire.

Usually, the railway units had the help of attached labour units, sometimes drawn from rear Allied troops but often oriental workers recruited especially for the job. Nor were railway troops only engaged in track laying. During the German offensives of early 1918, some units had to act as infantry. Luckily, unlike the British and some others, Canada had always maintained that all soldiers engaged on work at the front had to be trained as a basic infantry soldier first.

Throughout the course of the war, Canada eventually committed more and more railway troops. After the initial two companies, the contribution became 2 battalions, then 5, then 10 battalions, eventually reaching 13 battalions, 3 specialized companies and a railway shop company. Outside of the Western Front, a Canadian Railway Bridging Company was employed in the Middle East. The Director General Transportation (Construction) of the whole of the British Armies in France was Canadian Brigadier Jack Stewart. He formed an administrative HQ of Canadian Railway Troops at GHQ of the British and Empire armies, actually quite separate from Canadian Corps.

From April 1917 to end of the war, these units built 1,169 miles of track and 1,404 miles of light track. Each and every day there were 8,000 men employed on the construction of new track and 4,000 employed on maintenance of existing rail and tramlines. From 1917 to the end of the war, all light railway construction on the British front was done by Canadian troops and attached labour. Most of this work was done under conditions of enemy action and from 1 April 1917, to end of war, Railway Troops suffered 1,977 casualties.

Amenities were important to the troops. A number of private civilian organizations - the Salvation Army, the Knights of Columbus and the YMCA - established canteens and recreation centres for the soldiers. (CWM, CEF Album 3, 2154)

THE WOUNDED

*Wounded soldiers coming in from Vimy Ridge, 1917.
(CWM, CEF Album 2, 1435)*

An Advanced Dressing Station in the field. Note the presence of German prisoners. (CWM, CEF Album 6, 3309)

Treatment and care of the wounded was an escalating process. On the battlefield, first aid and assistance for evacuation was in the hands of unit comrades or, more likely, unit stretcher bearers. Casualties were evacuated to unit aid stations where the most basic treatment and triage was done by a Medical Officer, a doctor, and some assistants. Those that had a chance of survival were evacuated, normally by wagon or vehicle, sometimes carried by hand, to a brigade or divisional medical unit for further care. The more serious a case was, the further back the casualty was taken for more and more specialized medical care. Eventually, a casualty might be sent to a major medical facility near the English Channel, one major Canadian hospital being at Etaples. Some were taken to England.

Collection of wounded and dead was done under a flag of the Red Cross, normally by soldiers of the units engaged. Occasionally, a local truce might be arranged but mostly each side respected the medical personnel of the other.

German prisoners under guard treat each other's wounds, probably at a unit aid station behind the lines, before being moved to the rear to a POW collection point.

*Prisoners would be moved to the rear, in accordance with the Geneva Convention, out of harm's way. They were allowed to keep their helmets and respirators for self-protection, although in this case the prisoners appear to be devoid of most of their equipment. The youthfulness of most of the soldiers involved in the war is evident in the faces of both German and Canadian soldiers in this picture.
(CWM, CEF Album 6, 3799)*

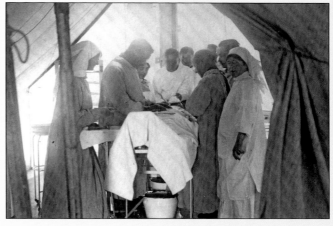

Medical advances were rapid in the First World War. Treatment for chemical wounds resulting from the use of gas munitions was one new challenge for military medicine. Whereas in previous conflicts the standard treatment for a range of severe wounds was amputation, the choice of protocols for doctors was greatly expanded as medical expertise grew.

The treatment of shell-shock was another major problem, one that is still being grappled with in modern times under various different names, such as post-traumatic stress.

Mechanization contributed to better evacuation and advances in medical techniques resulted in an increasingly improved medical system. It was common for soldiers to be medically treated and returned to duty, sometimes back into the front line more than once.

Sanitation and treatment of non-battle casualties also improved, saving many lives in comparison to previous wars.

Above left: Stretcher-bearers are deployed. The use of trucks became increasingly common. (CWM, CEF Album 4, 3308)
Medical operations were often carried out under canvas in rear areas. Nurses were normally emplyed there, not forward. (CWM, 19780067-034)

(CWM, CEF Album 1, 0626)

The divisional aid station pictured above survives today as mixed residential and commercial buildings (below) in the Belgian town of Vlamertinghe just west of Ypres.

More ambulances lined up at the back side of the building shown above.
(CWM, CEF Album 3, 2236)

Prime Minister Robert Borden reviewing the troops, with General Currie taking the salute. It was on such a visit to the front that Borden became convinced of the need to enact compulsory service to secure the replacements needed to keep the Canadian Corps up to full strength. The measure was enormously unpopular in Quebec, and in the end resulted in only some 25,000 men actually arriving in France, leading Canadian historians Jack Granatstein and David Bercuson to conclude that "As a military measure... conscription was at best a partial success; as a political measure, it was a longterm unmitigated failure...."

(NAC, PA-002746)

Lieutenant Alfred Theodore Joseph Bastien, "Canadian Gunners in the Mud, Passchendaele" *(CWM, 19710261-0093)*

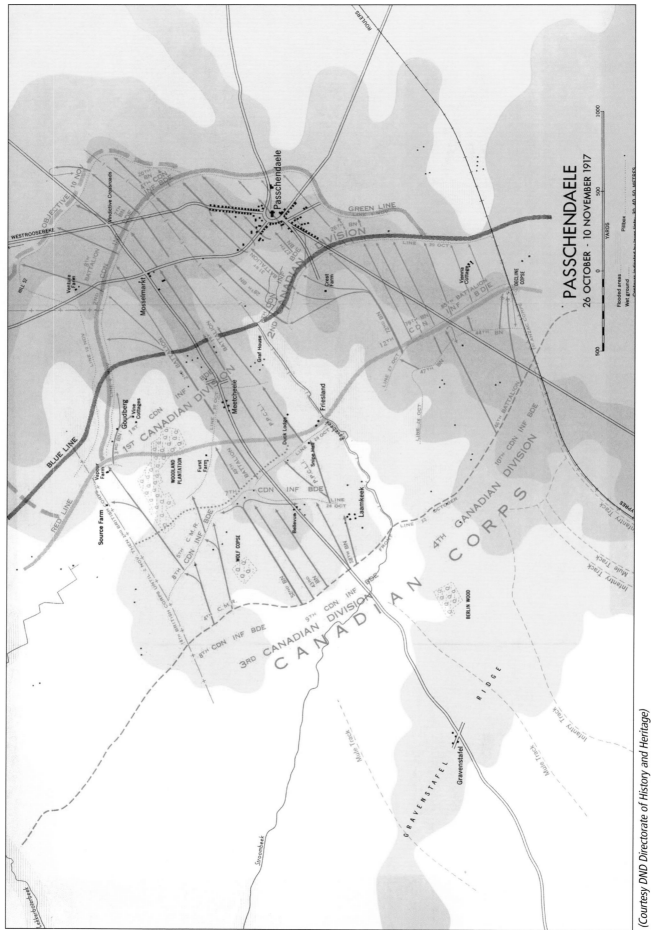

PASSCHENDAELE
26 OCTOBER - 10 NOVEMBER 1917

Flooded areas
Wet ground
Pillbox
Contours indicated by lines: datum 20, 40, 60 METRES

YARDS
500 0 500 1000

(Courtesy DND Directorate of History and Heritage)

PASSCHENDAELE

"We made gun positions at Passchendaele out of crates of bully beef. We, the infantry, assisted the engineers and the artillery in transporting tons of bully beef and pouring it into the mud until at last it had sunk deep enough to give a solid foundation for an eighteen-pounder gun."
Gregory Clark, 4th Canadian Mounted Rifles
CBC Radio, In Flanders Fields
Episode 10, "The Battle of Passchendaele"

(Below:)Generals Currie (left) and Haig. (CWM, CEF Album3, 2512)

(Above) Crest Farm memorial garden at Passchendaele.

In the fall of 1917, the Canadian Corps returned north to Flanders to partake in the Third Battle of Ypres, or the Battle of Passchendaele as Canadians more commonly know it, after the small town that stood on the top of the German-occupied ridge northwest of Ypres. The ridge and village had been the final objective of British operations in the Ypres Salient area since late July 1917.

In the opening phase operations, reminiscent to a degree of the Somme, British and ANZAC forces attacked repeatedly north and east of Ypres and made only modest gains in return for large casualty lists. In the process, some of the ground lost by Canadians in the St Julien and Gravenstafel areas in 1915 was re-captured. The ultimate prize, however, was the ridgeline upon which the small town of Passchendaele sat, about eight kilometres northeast of Ypres.

Exactly why the British High Command felt that the offensive was necessary is a matter of historical debate. The offensive was not fully supported by the British War Cabinet and later became a matter of recrimination between Field Marshal Haig and British Prime Minister Lloyd George. The British Admiralty had expressed its concerns about the Channel ports remaining in enemy hands and supported Haig's plan to push the German forces back from them. George and some politicians were skeptical of the handling of Empire troops. Moreover, Lloyd George disagreed with Haig and suggested that the casualties that would be incurred were neither desirable nor necessary. Haig later implied that the French had asked for offensive action in the latter part of 1917 to divert German attention from the southern French front to allow them to recover from exhaustion and mutinies in their army, but French sources later refuted this.

Whatever its origins, the Flanders offensive of 1917 eventually involved 51 British and Empire divisions in retaking some of the German-held high ground around the Ypres Salient.

The best place for the visitor today to view the Canadian part in the battle is the memorial garden at what was then Crest Farm, a German strongpoint just to the west of the village. Looking northwest from the garden one can look down at the two ridge spurs running from southwest to northeast. Modern roads run up the spine of each and these provide today's visitor an opportunity to move along in the general directions of advance of the attacking troops. At the bottom of the spurs, the Ravensbeek stream runs almost perpendicular to the heights and then northeast along the intervening valley. The start line for the first Canadian attacks was in the valley. The terrain of the north spur, the Bellevue spur, is clearly visible and one can pick out the actual and probable locations of some of the large German concrete emplacements that held up the advancing troops. Many of the pillboxes have been destroyed over the years but a few still remain, blended into civilian farms that have sprung up since the battle. The southern spur, the axis of advance for half of the Canadian Corps, is more difficult to discern because of tree growth and modern building. The church steeple rises above today's clean and modern town of Passchendaele as one looks to the northeast.

Waterloo pillbox at Paschendaele. (CWM, CEF Album 6, 4649)

In early October of 1917 General Currie and the Canadian Corps received orders to be prepared to move north to the Ypres Salient to join Second British Army's planned operations in Flanders. British and Empire forces had advanced to within a mile of Passchendaele but were now stalled and the weather had turned wet. The fighting had destroyed the low ground's agricultural drainage system and the battlefield was turning into soft mud. Attacks, primarily by the Australians, bogged down by mid-October attaining only intermediate objectives. The ridge and town were still tantalizingly just out of reach.

It was into this situation that the Canadian Corps was thrust. Ordered to move from the Lens sector, a reluctant General Currie expressed strong reservations about the possibility of success in the wet autumn over deteriorating ground conditions. However, the by-now experienced Canadian Corps staff had the planning process down almost to a science. An initial reconnaissance showed that about half of the battlefield was covered in water or mud. Currie was also unhappy with support arrangements, particularly engineer and artillery support, provided for the Corps' attack. Moreover, the German system of defence changed at this time so that forward lines were held lightly by an interlocking network of machinegun outposts, concrete shelters, and reserves that were able to counterattack quickly against any Allied gains. Currie pressed for and was granted time to make further dispositions and preparation for offensive action by the Canadian Corps. He planned a three-phase attack with intervals of a few days between each, rotating divisions in the lead for each phase. Knowing only too well by now the science of casualty prediction, Currie glumly forecast the cost at 16,000 Canadian casualties.

After thorough consideration and preparation, the Canadian Corps' Third and Fourth Divisions moved across their Start Lines and began the attack on 26 October. Flanked on the right by the Australian Corps and by British Fifth Army divisions on the left, each Canadian division moved up the parallel heights, following an axis marked by the roads that climbed over the back of the hills. Fighting was hard and attacks were hampered by mud, machine guns and rain. It often took individual acts of bravery at the lowest level to move units forward. By 28 October, the Canadians had consolidated on or near their interim objective, the Red Line, an advance of about 500 yards forward in the south to about 1,000 yards forward in the north. For the next few days, engineers rushed forward to lay planking and bridges and fill muddy craters so that mules could bring supplies forward.

On 30 October, the two leading Canadian divisions again struck at the defenders. From their current positions, the attackers were charged with making overall gains of 600-700 yards to their Blue Line objectives. Under a cold and rainy sky, and with massive artillery support, the Canadian divisions quickly worked their way forward. The Third Division on the north flank swept past defenders and outstripped their British support units as they moved deeper into German territory. On the Bellevue Spur, aggressive low-level infantry tactics took position after position. Hard fighting on the Fourth Division front resulted in the capture of the German strong point Crest Farm. Some patrols ventured as far as the outskirts of the village of Passchendaele itself. Because of large German counterattack forces detected forming in the area of Mosselmarkt, these weak Canadian forward elements were withdrawn and consolidated in brigade areas, but Canadian lead units were ordered to hold and defend. Subsequent attempts by German forces to re-take the areas were broken up by artillery and machine gun fire.

The stretch of road at right (and below today) backs on the eastern side of Tyne Cot Cemetary near Passchendaele.
(CWM, CEF Album 6, 4525)

One gets a feel for what the attacking Canadian infrantry saw in 1917: Passchendaele in the distance, and Germans on the high ground.

Three battalions of Canadian infantry from the Second Division moved so quickly from their positions just north of Crest Farm that they were inside the German artillery barrage and upon the Germans before those defenders could man their machine guns. Within three hours the village was taken. The attacking First Division battalions on the north flank encountered some difficulty because of swampy ground and enemy resistance. However, the main division attack swept quickly along the Bellevue Spur and up to Mosselmarkt. Within a few hours, the prize that had eluded the Allies for so many years was in Canadian hands.

After a week's pause at the Blue Line to allow a switch of divisions, and to let flanking British formations catch up, First and Second Divisions took their place in the line, ready to jump off at dawn on 6 November. Artillery support from the British on the northern flank and diversionary attacks by the Australians and British in the south began as the Canadians advanced.

On 10 November, the end game was played out as Second Division attacked the ridgeline and crossroads north of Passchendaele. Resistance was light in some areas but the attackers, being more concentrated than previously and now in a salient, suffered from heavy shelling and counter-attacks before they could push the German units and observation posts back down the far side of the ridge.

By this time it had been decided that the Flanders operations would cease in preparation for new British offensives in the Cambrai area. Accordingly, the Canadian Corps engaged in no more major offensive operations and was eventually relieved, beginning on 14 November. By 20 November, the Canadian Corps was back in the Lens-Vimy sector. Currie's prediction of 16,000 casualties was frighteningly accurate. The official history lists 15,654 battle casualties in the Passchendaele offensive.

Action photography at its 1917 best.: a shell bursts near a derelict tank. Note the mud and water.
(CWM 19801134-038)

The Canadian Corps is remembered in this signpost near the Crest Farm site of the Canadian Memorial to the fighting at Passchendaele.

Soldiers carrying wounded comrade at Passchendaele employing a crude, duck-board walkway typical of the frontline trenches of the time. (NAC, PA-002367)

Soldiers moving trench mats (duckboards) into the line at Passchendaele. (NAC, PA-002084)

"All you could see was shellholes with a group of men in them, and you could look perhaps two hundred yards over and see the Germans in the same position."
V.W. Odlum, Commander 11th Infantry Brigade
CBC Radio, In Flanders Fields
Episode 10, "The Battle of Passchendaele"

The combination of rain and an agricultural drainage system destroyed by artillery made for very tough slogging for the infantry-men on both sides. Soldiers employed ladder-like "trench mats" or duckboards to make for more efficient movement in the quagmire of mud that characterized the front-line trenches of Passchendaele. Most movement of troops and supplies took place under cover of darkness and hundreds of men died of drowning when they fell off a duck board into this morass of filth and mud. They were soaking wet all the time and it is reported that a man's greatcoat weighed in at a whopping 50 pounds.

Machine gunners at Passchendaele. (NAC, PA-002162)

Tyne Cot is the largest British Commonwealth War Graves Cemetery. It is a few kilometres southwest of Passchendaele and covers an area of some 3.5 hectares. Amongst the nearly 12,000 graves in it lay 966 Canadians. (Inset photo: Steve Douglas, Maple Leaf Legacy Project)

The panels across the back wall list the 33,783 British and other Commonwealth soldiers who fell in the Ypres sector with no known resting place. None of these are Canadians, who are listed instead on the Menin Gate in Ypres and at Vimy Ridge.

Sir Alfred James Munnings, "Charge of Flowerdew's Squadron" (CWM, 19710261-0443)

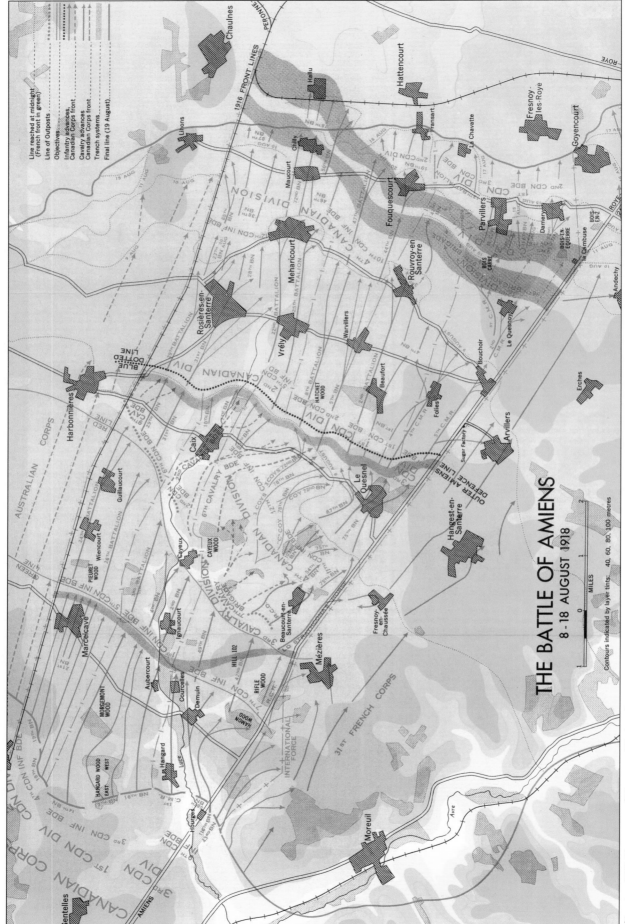

THE BATTLE OF AMIENS
8 - 18 AUGUST 1918

MILES

Contours indicated by layer tints: 40, 60, 80, 100 metres

(Courtesy DND Directorate of History and Heritage)

Private Donald Johnston McKinnon, No. 7 Platoon, 73rd Battalion, returning from the front line.   (NAC, PA-000867)

The general war situation had changed substantially by the beginning of 1918. The French were still recovering and re-organizing after serious mutinies in their forces, mainly as a result of an excess of offensive action along the front and especially at Verdun. Russia bowed out of the war in late 1917 as a result of internal revolution. Passchendaele had been costly for both the British Empire and for the Germans. The latter, however, were now in a position to transfer westward the many divisions no longer needed in the east. On the Italian front, German forces won large gains in the Caporetto area in November. The British attempt to mass tanks at Cambrai in November and December produced only mediocre gains and did not result in the expected breakthrough. Only in Palestine did the British enjoy success as Allenby's troops liberated Jerusalem in time for Christmas. On balance, the situation was somewhat grim for the Allies.

Canada had its own share of turmoil. Calls for conscription reached a crescendo across Canada and precipitated a political crisis. In the end, compulsory service was introduced to the chagrin of most people of Quebec and at the expense of many agricultural interests in western Canada. In Europe, Canadian demands for more autonomy in the administrative control and support of Canadian military forces began to agitate the British government. There was some disagreement also on the financial arrangements between the two countries for payment for troops, ammunition and supplies.

Germany too faced grim prospects. The numerical advantage remained with the western Allies, especially after the United States mobilized to join the war after the sinking of the *Lusitania* in April 1917. The Allied blockade of the Continent was slowly strangling the German economic base. The High Command decided to strike a decisive blow against the Allies on the Western Front in March 1918. Most of the initial assault was directed against the British sector with feint attacks against the French to the south.

On 10 March 1918, the Germans advanced across a broad front in the Somme area and attacked into and south of the Ypres Salient. The Somme offensive almost clove apart the British and French commands, as Paris was threatened again as in 1914. The German push in Flanders gained back areas they had only recently lost, including the high ground at Passchendaele that the Canadian Corps had so dearly won just months before.

The sector manned by the Canadian Corps around Lens was between the main German thrusts and as such was mostly unaffected. However, some other Canadian formations were involved. The Canadian Cavalry Brigade under British command took part in a sharp action southeast of Amiens. Finally freed from the confines of the trenches and able to exploit their mobility, horse-mounted troops were effective in stalling the advance of German units at Moreuil Wood at the end of March, their actions immortalized in the painting at the beginning of this chapter. Elsewhere, some Canadian infantry divisions were temporarily detached from the Canadian Corps to reinforce beleaguered British formations.

This caused some tactical difficulties for General Currie, who had to extend his remaining formations across a wide front to take up the slack. More importantly, the Canadians saw the loss of their divisions as a major command and control problem. The Canadian Corps was being denuded of its troops. At one time for a short period, the Corps Headquarters had no formations under its command. The British regarded this as merely moving about Empire troops not directly engaged at the moment to meet an emergency situation. But Currie protested firmly, pointing out that his Corps would fight better as an entity. The Canadian government representatives in the UK made clear to the British high command that the people of Canada expected their soldiers to be together.

Field Marshal Haig, obviously considering the Canadian divisions only as a source of needed reserves, was taken aback that Empire troops should expect to be treated as an integral whole, complaining that Canadians seemed to regard themselves "more as allies than as members of the British Empire." That was precisely the point: since Vimy Ridge, the Canadian Corps had seen themselves as exactly that.

The German 1918 Spring Offensive, after gaining large amounts of Allied territory and almost breaking through to the city of Amiens, finally petered out. Even though the Canadian Corps was not engaged as a single formation against the German offensive, casualties from March to July totaled approximately 9,000. Reunited in May with all its divisions and about 100,000 strong, the Corps was relieved from its positions near Lens and moved to a reserve position until July. Engineer units were reorganized, infantry units brought up to strength and machinegun units were reapportioned.

Now it was the turn of the Allies. Major counter-offensives, coordinated under the new Supreme Commander, the French Maréchal Ferdinand Foch, began in late July. The Canadian Corps received orders to move to the area of Amiens in the first week of August.

This was done with utmost secrecy under the cover of both darkness and an elaborate deception plan that indicated the Canadians would be employed in the Ypres area. By now German intelligence had learned to watch Canadian activities closely. They were able to detect only the disappearance of the Corps from their front and not an exact new destination. Two battalions of infantry plus medical and signal units were sent north to the Mount Kemmel area south of Ypres. Their mission was to be obvious and to mislead the enemy about the actual destination of the Corps. The ruse was partly successful but, more to the point, it was an indication of the interest generated among enemy intelligence wherever the Canadians went.

The main road from Amiens to Roye, and the railway from Amiens to Chaulnes, formed the flanks of the attack area of the Canadian Corps. The easiest way today to get a feel for the area is by taking the main road to Roye. Travelling away from Amiens you will see on the north side of the divided highway the memorial garden at Le Quesnel. This quiet and tranquil place, adjacent to the bustle of the main traffic, was on the path of the Canadian divisions as they moved quickly after the German troops in August 1918. A small cemetery at Hourges marks the approximate start line of the attack. Buried in the cemetery, too, are some of the Canadian cavalry soldiers who were killed earlier at Moreuil Wood, visible on the hill to the south.

The Canadian Corps moved across that start line at twenty minutes past four in the morning of 8 August. The leading troops wore light fighting order, having left their heavy packs and baggage behind them. The weather was fine and there was no moon. Some mist lingered in low areas.

Three Canadian divisions moved southeast in line abreast formation. The attack formations were different now, a recognition of the terrain to their front and the advances in military technology that helped them along their way. There were five waves of infantry. The first was a line of skirmishers whose main job was to screen the advance, flush out the enemy and identify positions. After that came three lines of infantry but, instead of being strung out shoulder to shoulder, they moved in small columns of about section strength, ready to move flexibly in accordance with more general mission-type orders. The last wave consisted of carrying parties, moving up additional ammunition, machineguns, grenades and defensive stores, and ready to carry back information, prisoners and casualties. A large artillery barrage preceded the moving men.

"You had the feeling that everything was well planned, well organized. People knew what they were about, the staff was on the job. Everything seemed to go like clockwork..."
G.S. Rutherford, 52nd Battalion
CBC Radio, In Flanders Fields
Episode 14, "Amiens and Arras"

The photo above is the general position of the Start Line for Canadian Corps units in the Amiens attack, 8 August 1918, near the village of Hourges. The same location (right) is now the site of a Commonwealth War Graves Commission cemetery. (CWM, CEF Album 6, 4627)

Canadian infantry had worked with tanks as early as late 1916 on the Somme, when they had been introduced to the battlefield. Here a unit trains with a tank. Tanks were allocated to the Canadian Corps during the Amiens offensive in August 1918 and later as they moved eastward in the Hundred Days. (CWM, CEF Album 4, 03337)

The view of the ground looking out from Le Quesnel memorial clearly shows the rolling and undulating terrain in the region. Artillery moved forward quickly to keep enemy targets within range. Aircraft allocated to the Corps flew overhead to lay smoke, relay messages and to spot for artillery units. Co-operation with aircraft had mixed results, depending upon the level of prior training among units and the presence of mist in the mornings. Some aircraft were able to harass enemy units and positions in depth.

Le Quesnel memmorial (right) east of Amiens. The village of Le Quesnoy can be seen in the distance. It was here that the offensive ground to a halt.

The leading divisions of the Canadian Corps each had 42 tanks in support. Infantry often preceded them across obstacles and a number were lost due to mechanical or mobility problems in the marshy ground in intervening river valleys, particularly on the south flank in the Third Division area. Some tanks were designated to be support vehicles carrying mobile machinegun detachments forward. Unfortunately, some of the passengers got sick from the motion and the fumes and could not continue. Other tanks carried wire, pickets, ammunition and other supplies. The tank strength quickly declined but those that remained accomplished good work supporting the infantry.

Locre village in ruins - looking towards Mount Kemmel. Canadian units fought here as part of deception operations. (CWM, CEF Album 6, 4676)

This battle was one of the few when cavalry was launched in the offensive. The Canadian Cavalry Brigade and two companies of light tanks, part of the 3rd (British) Cavalry Division, and the 32nd British Division, were given to the Canadian Corps for operational employment during the battle. Canadian horsemen covered the right flank and, in concert with motorized machine gun batteries and cyclists, advanced over the open ground until blocked by Germans dug in with machine guns.

Canadian infantry often overran German units in their dugouts, so violent was the artillery preparation and so rapid the infantry advance. By the end of the first day, the bulk of the Canadian objectives to a line spanning Le Quesnoy - Caix - Harbonnières were firmly in hand. For a cost of less than 4,000 casualties, the Canadian Corps advanced eight miles. The Australians on the northern flank advanced seven. Other French and British formations moved between two and fives miles ahead. German units lost about 27,000 killed, wounded and captured. German General Eric Ludendorff described 8 August as the "Black Day" of the German army. His recommendation two days later to the Kaiser was to commence negotiations for peace.

On 9 August, the Fourth Canadian Division was committed to battle to overcome resistance that was stiffening in the area of the village of Le Quesnoy. This done, the other three divisions, later joined by the 32nd British Division under Canadian command, continued the fighting advance the next day, encountering deep defensive trench systems the farther east they went. By the third day, the forward troops began to run into some of the old Somme front defences that had been re-worked by the German army. A lull fell over the fighting on 12 August and further operations in the next week were minor by comparison, mostly to establish a new front line by 19 August.

The final tally was impressive. The Canadian Corps had met and bettered 15 German divisions, four of which ceased to exist. Penetration into enemy territory encompassed a depth of 14 miles on a front of just under six miles. More than 9,000 prisoners had been taken along with guns and mortars. The Canadians had sustained 11, 822 casualties. Described as "the shock army of the British Empire" by one author, the Canadian Corps had been instrumental in breaking through the German lines. The name, "The Hundred Days", refers to the period between 8 August and the final armistice on 11 November. The Battle of Amiens, 8 to 18 August, 1918, was the beginning of the end.

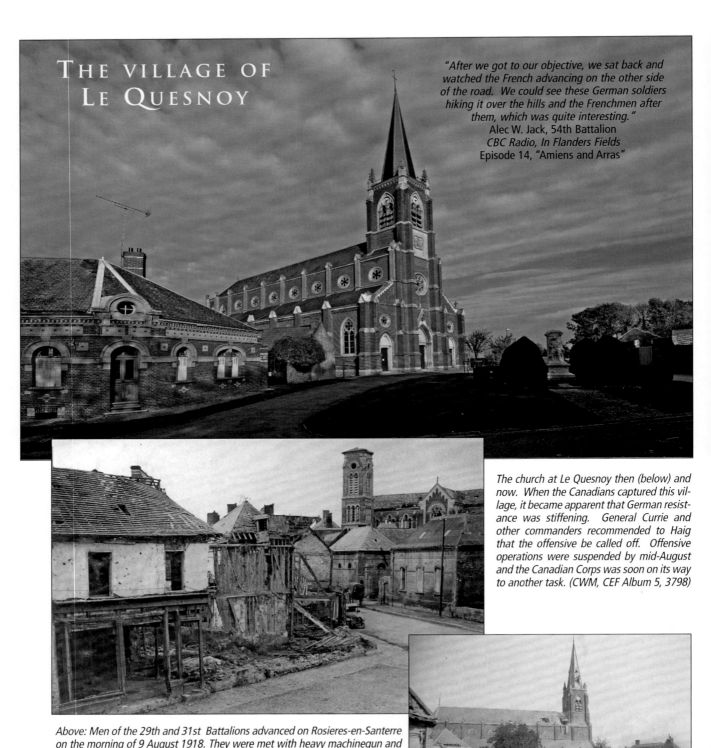

THE VILLAGE OF
LE QUESNOY

"After we got to our objective, we sat back and watched the French advancing on the other side of the road. We could see these German soldiers hiking it over the hills and the Frenchmen after them, which was quite interesting."
Alec W. Jack, 54th Battalion
CBC Radio, In Flanders Fields
Episode 14, "Amiens and Arras"

The church at Le Quesnoy then (below) and now. When the Canadians captured this village, it became apparent that German resistance was stiffening. General Currie and other commanders recommended to Haig that the offensive be called off. Offensive operations were suspended by mid-August and the Canadian Corps was soon on its way to another task. (CWM, CEF Album 5, 3798)

Above: Men of the 29th and 31st Battalions advanced on Rosieres-en-Santerre on the morning of 9 August 1918. They were met with heavy machinegun and artillery fire. Eventually the 31st Battalion was able to flank the village to the south. (CWM, CEF Album 6, 4624)

AMIENS CATHEDRAL

TO THE GLORY OF GOD
AND IN MEMORY
OF THE OFFICERS
NON-COMMISSIONED OFFICERS
AND MEN
OF THE ROYAL CANADIAN DRAGOONS
WHO GAVE UP THEIR LIVES
FOR THE CAUSE OF RIGHT AND LIBERTY
DURING THE GREAT WAR
1915 · 1916 · 1917 · 1918

ERECTED BY THEIR COMRADES
IN THE REGIMENT

A LA GLOIRE DE DIEU
ET A LA MÉMOIRE
DES OFFICIERS SOUS-OFFICIERS ET SOLDATS
DU ROYAL CANADIAN DRAGOONS
QUI ONT DONNÉ LEUR VIE
POUR LA CAUSE DU DROIT ET DE LA LIBERTÉ
DANS LA GRANDE GUERRE
1915 · 1916 · 1917 · 1918

ÉRIGÉ PAR LEURS CAMARADES
DU RÉGIMENT

Now a UNESCO World Heritage Site, as the tallest and foremost example of French gothic architecture, the Cathedral of Notre Dame of Amiens is in the centre of the city that was the target of the German 1918 Spring Offensive. Inside the cathedral is a plaque commemorating Allied units that took part in the defence of the city. Among them is a plaque remembering the role of the Royal Canadian Dragoons, part of the Canadian Cavalry Brigade operating with the British Cavalry Division in Fourth Army. After the Germans were defeated by the French and US troops at the Second Battle of the Marne, the British launched an offensive east of Amiens. The Canadian Corps and the Australian Corps led the way.

(CWM, CEF Album 2, 1434)

(CWM, CEF Album 2, 1104)

MISERY

(CWM, CEF Album 2, 1100)

Rubble heaps that were villages dotted the landscape. In the case of aptly-named village of Misery, the central calvary in the town was put to use as a route marker signpost. The Canadian Corps would have probably passed via this road when it moved from the Amiens front and travelled north to take up positions preparatory to the final offensive from Arras eastward.

Churches and religious markers are often re-built in Europe on the same locations when they were destroyed. Remarkably, when photographing sites for this book, a calvary was discovered at the central intersection of the village of Misery. The chances of coincidence seemed to be too great. This was probably the same village our First World War phtographer passed through in 1918.

(CWM, CEF Album 2, 1099)

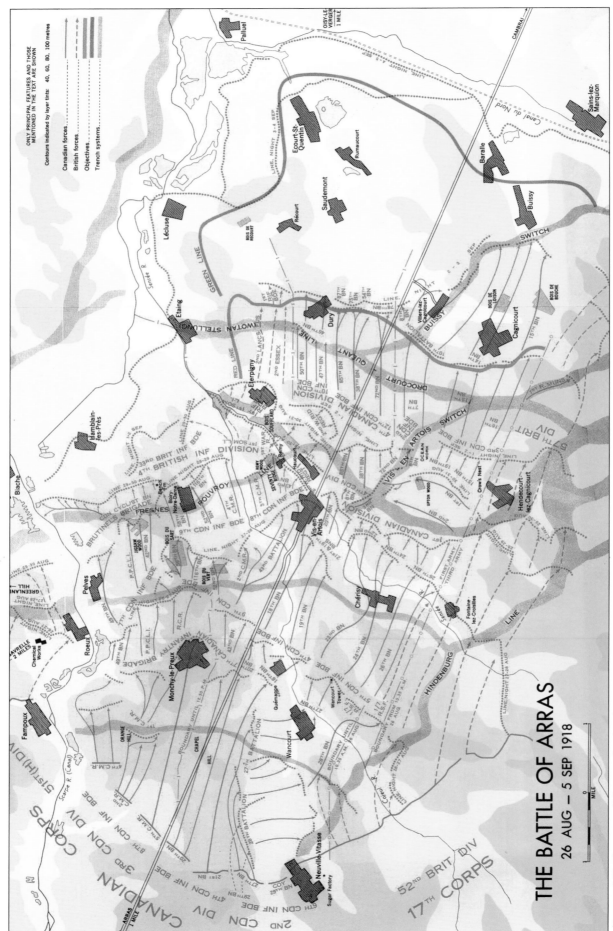

THE BATTLE OF ARRAS
26 AUG – 5 SEP 1918

(Courtesy DND Directorate of History and Heritage)

Arras, Canal du Nord & Cambrai

Sunrise on the Arras-Cambrai Road.

Events began to move quickly for the Canadian Corps as the Allies continued to press the German army. By the last week in August, shifted back north almost to its earlier position just east of Arras, the Corps received orders to attack along the Arras-Cambrai road, another old straight Roman road. The German tactic was to trade space for time with a view to imposing attrition on advancing Allied troops before making a stand at the so-called Hindenburg Line. The part of that strong defensive line facing the Canadian Corps was in the area just east of Vis-en-Artois near Dury. The official history calls this the Battle of Arras, but it is commonly known as the fight for the Drocourt-Quéant Switch, so named for the change in angle of orientation of the German defence lines.

Various hills and ridges, some rising sixty or more metres above the road level, dominate the ground along the highway. Additionally, two rivers intersect the direction of advance almost at right angles and had to be crossed, again mostly under plain observation from German trenches. The present-day monument to the actions fought by the Corps in this area is at Dury, near where the German lines were. It is a pleasant park, somewhat plain but surrounded by many maple trees in commemoration of the Canadian lives lost in the battle.

The efficiency of the Canadian Corps can be plainly seen in the ability of the formation to withdraw from positions in the line after the Battle of Amiens, move its support and fighting forces to just east of Arras, and then launch a major offensive involving all its divisions against an entrenched enemy, all within about a week. The staff work required for such a move alone is a major undertaking. Drawing up offensive plans and then executing them require enormous amounts of planning, preparation and logistical support. Lastly, to execute those plans calls for a high degree of battlefield ability. It is evident that the Canadian Corps as an entity had come a long way from the disorganized crew that had sailed from Quebec in 1914.

With a combination of heavy artillery preparation and simultaneous manoeuvring of battalions, the Second and Third Canadian Divisions pushed off on 26 August along each side of the highway. High ground in the northern sector near Monchy-le-Preux was taken and river crossings over the Cojeul River in the south were quickly established. By the night of 28 August, the First and Fourth Canadian Divisions relieved the two tired initial attackers and prepared to resume the advance toward the German positions proper. The Corps practised what was now quickly becoming the Canadian (and also Allied) way of war - to seize limited and attainable objectives rather than conduct massive offensives across the whole front.

"Well, of course, we never had any idea of another major attack in
eighteen days after the first attack,
but that's what we found we were for."
Alex Ross, 6th Infantry Brigade
CBC Radio, In Flanders Fields
Episode 14, "Amiens and Arras"

ARRAS

Ruins of Arras and the same street today (left). (CWM, CEF Album 2, 1313)

(Inset) Sam Hughes tours the ruins of Arras. (CWM, CEF Album 1, 0671)

A halt was called to make final preparations for the attack. Everyone clearly recognized the trenches opposite, the so-called Drocourt-Queant Switch, as one of the pivotal enemy positions of the Western Front. The enemy also knew the importance of his works and that an offensive was just a matter of time. German raiders and outposts pushed forward into Canadian positions to disrupt preparations for the imminent attack, to the degree that some units were still fighting for their jumping off lines when the Canadian Corps began its advance at first light on 2 September.

Supported by artillery and tanks and flanking British formations, the First Division and the Fourth Division surged forward. Fourth Division experienced heavy fighting on the northern flank but the First Division had better success in the south, penetrating deeply into the German positions by late night on 2 September. By day's end, parts of the German trench line were in Canadian hands and Currie gave orders for an advance by three divisions the next day to seize the remaining heights and defence works overlooking the Canal du Nord. A heavy battle was avoided when German units began to retire and soon the complete Corps was advancing against light opposition. The Corps consolidated its positions, adjusted its deployment and awaited the next battle. It was not long in coming.

The Hindenberg Line (right, CWM, CEF Album 6, 3392) was a massive obstacle comprised mainly of barbed wire entanglements and machine gun nests. The view below from the west edge of Monchy-le-Preux looks out from the German positions toward the Canadian lines.

Above: Sunrise bathes the Arras-Cambrai Road today.

The picture left was taken on 29 September 1918. The two Canadian soldiers are from the 75th Battalion and, in company with their German prisoner who does not seem overly upset about being captured, the men are near the village of Raillencourt, just west of the city of Cambrai. The milestone clearly identifies the location below. (CWM, CEF Album 4, 3326)

ARRAS–CAMBRAI ROAD

Busy section of the Arras Cambrai Road.
(CWM, CEF Album 4, 3147)

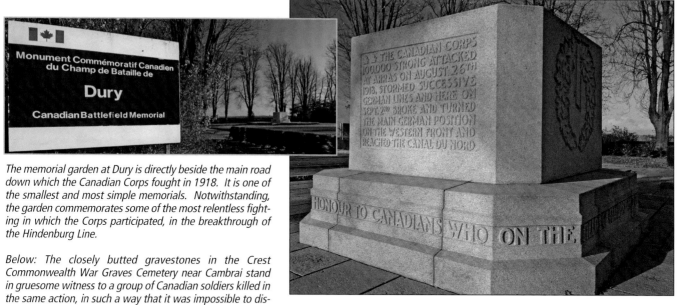

The memorial garden at Dury is directly beside the main road down which the Canadian Corps fought in 1918. It is one of the smallest and most simple memorials. Notwithstanding, the garden commemorates some of the most relentless fighting in which the Corps participated, in the breakthrough of the Hindenburg Line.

Below: The closely butted gravestones in the Crest Commonwealth War Graves Cemetery near Cambrai stand in gruesome witness to a group of Canadian soldiers killed in the same action, in such a way that it was impossible to distinguish their remains.

CANAL DU NORD

Canadian engineers build bridges across the Canal du Nord. In the picture above, note the hasty pontoon bridge that has been erected on the left with the sign, "Bridge For Horse Transport Only". A substantial bridge has already been built and this engineer effort will increase the mobility of the Corps' following administrative tail. These bridges are being built after the assault has passed forward and not under fire. Most bridges, of course, had been destroyed as part of German defensive preparations at the Canal du Nord, as well as other rivers and canals. Once on the far side of the obstacle, the Canadian Corps continually had to move massive amounts of ammunition, supplies and following units in a steady stream to maintain the momentum of the attack. (CWM, CEF Album 5, 3576)

After a reorganization of its resources in early 1918, the Canadian Corps had three times the number of engineers found in a British corps, almost 3,000. Each of the four divisions also had a separate bridging unit. More and centralized control of engineers meant better mobility when the war changed from one of trench-bound positional warfare to more open manoeuvre. (CWM, CEF Album 5, 3536)

However, the canal was not completely finished with part of it just east of the village of Inchy-en-Artois under construction and still dry. Taking a tremendous risk, Currie funneled his whole assault force through the relatively narrow defile of the dry canal bed. In doing so, the possibility existed that well-placed and well-timed German artillery concentrations would slaughter the tightly packed Canadians within the narrow confines of the canal as they moved forward.

The Canal du Nord and Bourlon Wood were two main obstacles that stood between the newly won ground and the city of Cambrai. Strong trench positions, barbed wire and machineguns covered every inch of territory over which the Canadian troops would have to traverse to move farther east. Accordingly, movement of troops by day was restricted as preparations commenced for the attack.

Correctly noting that Bourlon Wood was key terrain to capture, the British army commander assigned this to the Canadian Corps. To get to this stronghold, the Corps had to move over the major obstacles of deliberately flooded swamps and the canal itself, both of which ran perpendicular across the Canadian axis of advance.

The gamble worked, in spite of the difficulties. Artillery was carefully sited and designated batteries were ready to move forward quickly as assault battalions moved through the gap. Heavy artillery, for the first time, planned for moving barrages as had become the norm with field artillery. Engineers, recently re-organized in the Corps to provide more battlefield mobility, moved well forward to work with the lead assault troops. Other engineers had the tasks of improving seized crossings or throwing up bridges in other sectors for follow-on elements. To ensure the element of surprise so necessary in this instance, no preliminary bombardment disturbed the dawn overcast sky as, at 5:20 a.m. on 27 September, Canadian infantry broke forward from their nighttime assembly areas, debouched from the narrow lanes across the obstacle and fanned out, supported by artillery and tanks, onto a front almost 10 kilometres wide.

BOURLON

The Bourlon memorial.

The capture of the town and the woods to the south of Bourlon was key to the taking of Cambrai, a battle that General Currie considered to be one of the finest fought by the Canadian Corps.

Bourlon Church now (above) and then (below). (CWM, CEF Album 4, 3428)

By mid-morning Bourlon Wood was flanked, but stubborn German resistance in some parts of the enemy line prolonged the fighting into the evening. Rather than consolidate for the period of darkness in normal fashion, Currie ordered the troops to continue pressing throughout the night and the next day. His aim was to move units around the north side of Cambrai to prevent the enemy from consolidating new defensive works. Successive units and formations were fed into the battle that raged for another four days. Every hill and every village was a stongpoint and each had to be contested.

Finally, a four-division attack was ordered on 1 October to make Cambrai untenable. Limited objectives were seized, but only just so in a number of places. Battalions and brigades struggled to take their assigned objectives, often becoming intertwined in the process, the result of stubborn defence by opposing German forces. Because of the strong opposition and the fatigue of the Canadian divisions that had been engaged in hard fighting for five days, the offensive was halted.

The memorial at Bourlon Wood, on the west side of that key high terrain, is approachable only by a series of terraced steps among huge and very old trees. The climb for the military tourist is reminiscent of the uphill struggles that Canadian units often found themselves to be undertaking in this and similar operations on that part of the front.

By any measure, the attacks had been a success. A major obstacle had been breached. Cambrai was now under direct observation and fire, and some units had penetrated into the outskirts of the city. Over 7,000 prisoners and 200 guns had been captured from nine full German divisions and parts of three further formations. The Canadian Corps had protected the flanks of Third and Fourth British Armies in their respective offensives and the Corps had contributed greatly to the general Allied push eastward.

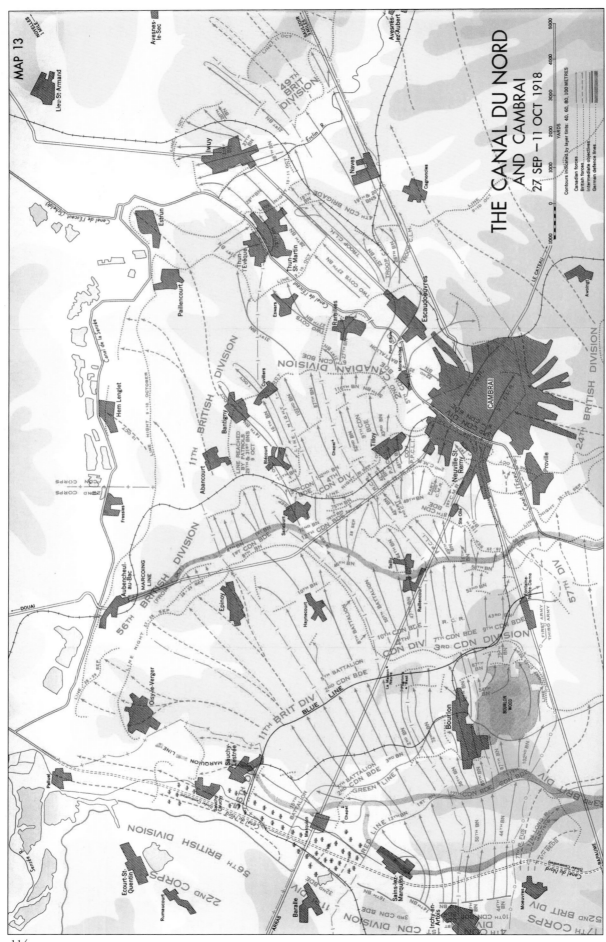

MAP 13

THE CANAL DU NORD
AND CAMBRAI
27 SEP – 11 OCT 1918

Contours indicated by layer tints: 40, 60, 80, 100 METRES
Canadian forces
British forces
Intermediate objectives
German defence lines

0   1000   2000   3000   4000   5000
YARDS

0   1000   METRES

114

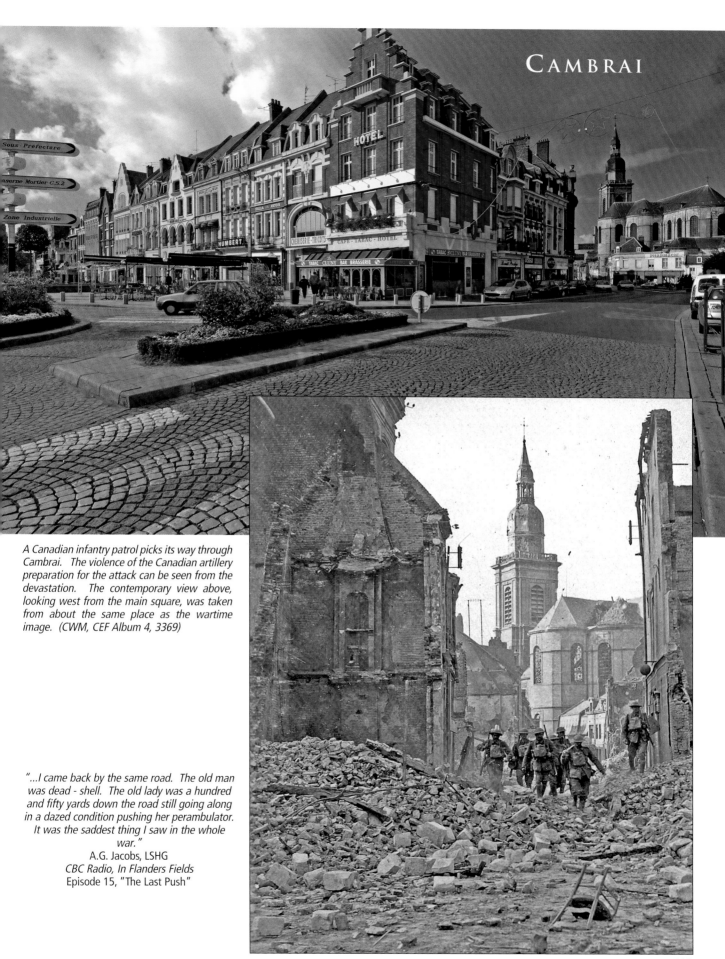

A Canadian infantry patrol picks its way through Cambrai. The violence of the Canadian artillery preparation for the attack can be seen from the devastation. The contemporary view above, looking west from the main square, was taken from about the same place as the wartime image. (CWM, CEF Album 4, 3369)

"...I came back by the same road. The old man was dead - shell. The old lady was a hundred and fifty yards down the road still going along in a dazed condition pushing her perambulator. It was the saddest thing I saw in the whole war."
A.G. Jacobs, LSHG
CBC Radio, In Flanders Fields
Episode 15, "The Last Push"

CAMBRAI

"You could see Cambrai burning for days before you ever got near, the fires the Germans had started."
Doug Oliver, 18th Battalion
CBC Radio, In Flanders Fields
Episode 15, "The Last Push"

(Above) The main square in Cambrai burns, a result of the recent fighting, as a Canadian patrol moves through the city. (CWM, CEF Album 4, 3393-4)

(Below) Thunderclouds form over the rebuilt main square in Cambrai today,
reminiscent of the fires of destruction in the archive picture.

On 8 and 9 October, Canadian forces in conjunction with British army units from the south took Cambrai proper. In the following two days, the Canadians, with some British units under their command, moved the Allied line beyond the Erclin River, some six or seven kilometres east of Cambrai itself. By 11 October, the Canadian Corps was relieved. The cost in killed, wounded and missing in action had topped 31,000 Canadians all ranks since 22 August. In return, the Germans had suffered the defeat of about 30 divisions, the loss of just fewer than 19,000 prisoners, 371 guns and almost 200 machineguns.

More importantly, the Canadian Corps had shown itself to be a strong and capable formation. It had manoeuvred well in this new brand of mobile warfare, so different from static trench life. Its tactics were sound and it had the capability to command other formations and units efficiently. General Currie, in giving his assessment later, suggested that the major Canadian memorial of the First World War should be emplaced not at Vimy Ridge but in the Cambrai area, so important did he think the battle to be. Other opinions prevailed, however, and the fighting for the Drocourt-Quéant Switch, Cambrai and the Canal du Nord are commemorated more simply by only the monumental gardens at Dury and Bourlon Wood.

Officers and men, and some civilians, kneel on chairs in the ruins of Cambrai cathedral to celebrate Thanksgiving 1918. The wreckage of war is evident although the side altar area and chandeliers seem to have escaped complete destruction. This is clearly a lull in the fighting which had moved past the area by this time, but the soldiers all have their gas masks with them nevertheless. (CWM, CEF Album 4, 03421)

The Cathedral is still one of the central buildings in Cambrai today. The side alter and the chairs have changed little, outwardly at least. The principal ornamentation of the knave is identical to that in the original picture and only some wall decoration has changed. Of course, all the damage has been repaired and the cathedral is used by civilians now.

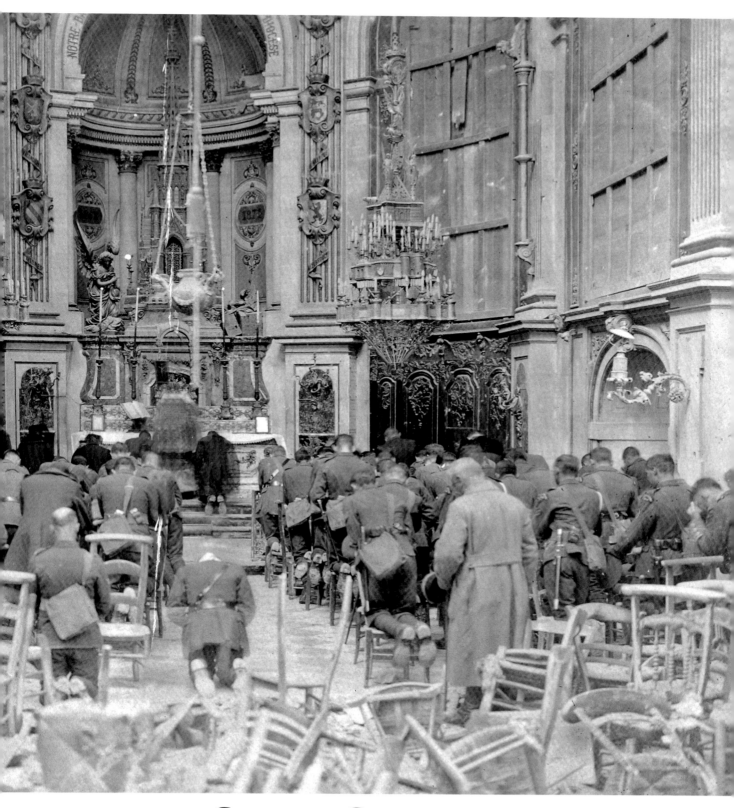

CAMBRAI CATHEDRAL

INGLIS SHELDON-WILLIAMS 1920.
MONS. NOV. 11TH 1918.

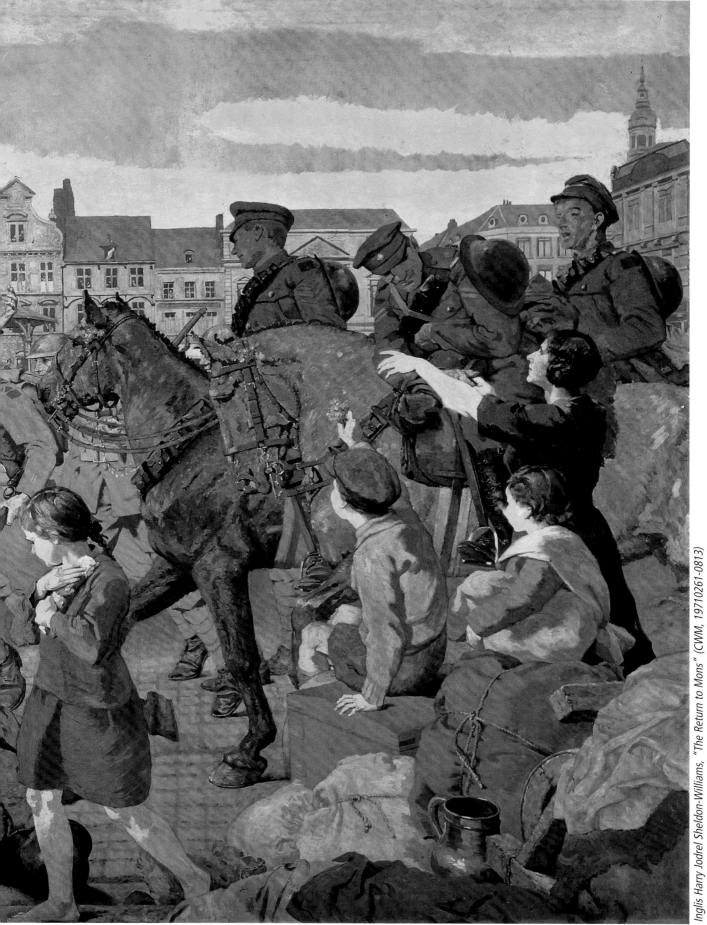

Inglis Harry Jodrel Sheldon-Williams, "The Return to Mons" (CWM, 1971026I-0813)

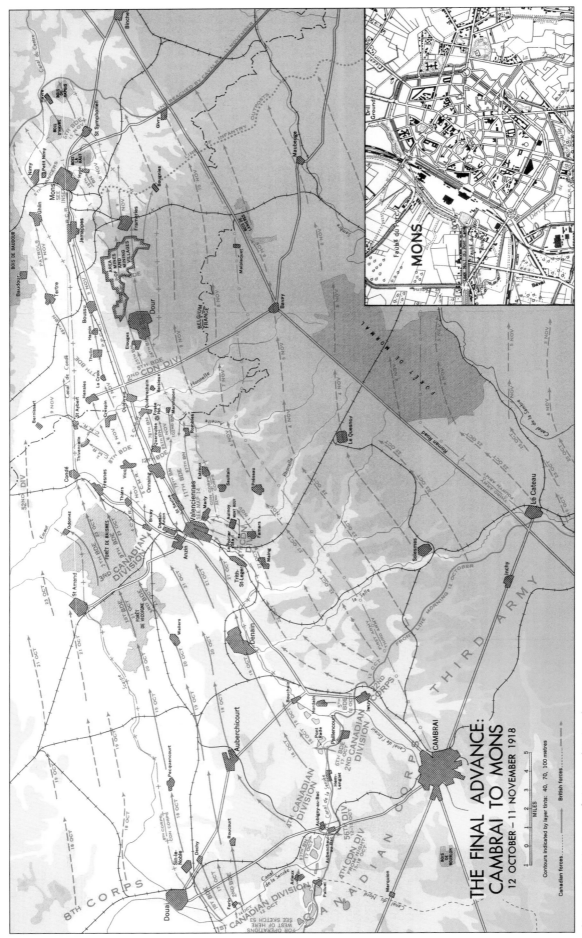

THE FINAL ADVANCE: CAMBRAI TO MONS
12 OCTOBER – 11 NOVEMBER 1918

Contours indicated by layer tints: 40, 70, 100 metres

MILES
0 1 2 3 4 5

Canadian forces ········
British forces ——————

MONS

(Courtesy DND Directorate of History and Heritage)

THE FINAL PUSH, OCCUPATION & HOME

November 11th celebrations in Mons. (CWM, CEF Album 5, 3618)

When the Canadian Corps came out of the line on 11 October, little did the soldiers at the time realize this would prove to be exactly one month before an Armistice would take effect. Despite the rumours about peace negotiations that had started to circulate, the average Canadian soldier knew that some stiff fighting surely still lay ahead. While German forces were withdrawing in some areas, in others they were making the Allied advance a costly venture. The First Canadian Division, temporarily under the command of the British 22nd Corps, had advanced to the Canal de la Sensée along a line north of Arleux.

On 17 October, the German front went quiet. It soon became clear that a general enemy withdrawal was underway. Following the Cambrai-Mons road, beginning on a line from Douai to Cambrai, the Canadian Corps pushed ahead. Optimistically, armoured cars, a battalion of cyclists and a squadron of cavalry were allocated to each of the lead two divisions in the hope of moving quickly against a retreating enemy.

The advance again was the new, open kind of warfare, starkly in contrast to the static trench warfare of the previous years. Now a major problem was to move supplies and ammunition forward quickly enough to match the advancing lead elements. As well, there were refugees to contend with, many of whom had to be tended medically, fed and diverted off main routes that had to be kept clear for supply columns. The refugee problem eased somewhat as the troops moved farther east into former German rear areas where the population had been less disrupted by the occupation.

As more and more Allied troops pushed the Germans back, the front began to narrow and the Canadian Corps' next mission became defined. By 22 October, forward troops were at the St Amand-Valenciennes road. It was obvious that the town of Valenciennes and the large forested area to its north would be the next attack objectives.

Third Division assumed the vanguard of the Corps from the First Division and cleared the forest, some 7,000 yards of wooded area, by 23 October. Canadian troops reached the River Escaut, consolidated the line and probed for bridgeheads, pausing to allow flanking formations to catch up to their advance. The problem of Germans in the town of Valenciennes remained and preparations began to attack the garrisons there. On the high ground of Mont Houy just to the south of the city, German defensive positions blocked further movement of the Canadians and the Allies on that flank.

A preliminary attack by the British on 28 October failed to seize the Mont Houy area. On 1 November, two brigades of the Fourth Canadian Division attacked with massive artillery support. The operation was complicated by the fact that there were a large number of French civilians in the city and supporting fire had to be carefully planned. Under the weight of the barrages, the Canadians advanced in a pincer movement from the south and from the northeast. During the first day, Canadian units penetrated the city and completed the encirclement from the north. By nightfall, the objectives were secured and fresh troops were moved through the attacking formations to push on eastward. Loss of civilian life was kept to a minimum by careful planning and execution.

VALENCIENNES

Valenciennes railway station was seized by Canadians as they swept into the city.   (CWM, CEF Album 5, 3563)

From 2 November onward, there was no major or prolonged engagement for the Canadian Corps. British General Headquarters cancelled a general attack order for 3 November when it became apparent that only weak German rearguards remained. Instead, a broad general advance was ordered across the front. With two divisions forward, the Canadians moved east. Immediately, they ran into two problems.

Weather, until now often not in favour of the Allies, turned wet again. Rain complicated the already extended logistical lines. Some low-lying areas near the numerous rivers and streams were flooded and extra engineer effort was needed to maintain even basic mobility. Some areas had to be skirted. Troops became fatigued by the effort of moving, marching and being continually outside in the rain.

The second difficulty, as always, was the German resistance. Although the enemy army was withdrawing, it was a fighting withdrawal. Particularly when the French-Belgian border was reached, more and more sharp battles were fought, albeit on a lesser scale than previously because of the depleted state of German units. Roads were cratered, bridges demolished and booby-traps and mines were planted by the retreating troops. In some places, various units carried out a very credible defence from strong positions. The towns of Vicq and Quarouble, and the Petite and Grande Honnelle Rivers, among others, posed serious obstacles to the Canadian battalions pushing forward.

By 7 November, the Canadian Corps had passed into Belgium and continued on either side of the main Cambrai road toward Mons. Fourth Division reached that city's outskirts by nightfall on 9 November. Troops from the Second Division closed up along the south of the city limits on the same day, having moved quickly against light opposition in the last few kilometres of their sector. Such swift movement, however, was not to remain the case.

Throughout 10 November and into the night, the closer the Canadians got to Mons, the more intense became the reply to forward movement or probing patrols from German defenders. Movement was further complicated by a number of canals throughout the city. But by dawn on 11 November, the city was generally in Canadian hands.

Mopping up was continuing to the eastern outskirts. British cavalry patrols and 6 Canadian Brigade moved east of Mons up to the Canal du Centre to occupy the villages, woods and high ground there. At 6:30 a.m. a message was received announcing an armistice would take effect at 11:00 a.m. that day, 11 November 1918. Fighting gradually diminished during the morning as troops on both sides received the word.

The hodge-podge of older buildngs in front of the rebuilt Valenciennes city hall has been replaced with modern clutter.
CWM, CEF Album3538)

"So Price said, 'Let's go outside and see what's going on outside here.' So the two of us went outside, and all of a sudden, bang! One shot came from way up the end of the street, got him right through the back and through the heart and he fell dead right in my arms there."
A.B Goodmurphy, 28th Battalion
CBC Radio, In Flanders Fields
Episode 16, "Victory"

One of the places liberated on the morning of 11 November was the village of St Symphorien, southeast of Mons. The location of a small cemetery in which some of the first British casualties of the war in August 1914 had been buried., it also became the resting place of Private George Price, the last Canadian soldier killed in action, shot by a sniper as he crossed a street two minutes before the ceasefire took effect at 11:00 a.m. His gravestone is pictured at right, with a flag recently left by a Canadian tourist.

MONS

The Armistice meant rest to these tired soldiers of the
42nd Battalion in Mons. (CWM, CEF Album 5, 3655)

The archival picture below was taken in Mons during the victory parade held there four days after the Armistice. Each liberated French town was anxious to show its gratitude and often a parade with representative units of the formations that fought in the area was organized. Architecturally, little has changed in this beautiful square today.

Allied artillery units fired final salvoes as the hour of the armistice approached. One German machine gunner fired off a complete belt of ammunition in one last gesture while others sent up flares to mark the occasion. Generally, a silence descended upon the battlefield as guns stopped for the first time in four years. The general mood of the troops was one of weary reflection, a distinct contrast to the celebrations that sent crowds spilling into the streets in cities farther behind the lines.

(CWM, CEF Album 5, 3674)

The day following the "victory" parade, elements of the First and Second Divisions began moving toward the Rhine River bridges at Cologne and Bonn respectively, 250 miles away, where they would share occupation duties in Germany. The progress was slow, partly due to the rainy and cold weather from the 25th onward, and partly to allow the German army time to deposit their arms into designated dumping areas and to return its soldiers to the Fatherland.

Along the way, supplies were moved with great difficulty and troops were kept in operational readiness. Before the symbolic crossing of the Rhine, units were held in assembly areas to prepare themselves and their equipment for the historic entry. Thus, it was not until the morning of 4 December that the Canadians crossed in review order, bayonets fixed, in pouring rain.

The military duties of the occupation force consisted mainly of control of movement of civilians into and out of occupation zones. For most Germans, the Allied troops were a symbolic reminder of defeat for Germany. For most of the Canadians, their main thought was to return to Canada.

(CWM, CEF Album 3, 2140]

After a short period of occupation, in January 1919 the First and Second Divisions rejoined the other divisions and Corps troops that had remained in Belgium. From there, the Corps began moving throughout February and March to the UK. General Currie, against considerable political opposition, fought successfully to have all units of the Canadian Corps returned to Canada, via England, as the formed units in which they had fought.

An efficient system of Dispersal Camps took care of the paperwork and expedited the final clearances necessary when soldiers and units entrained for their home unit station in Canada. Most units were back in Canada by mid-1919.

*"You can probably put yourself in our position.
Myself, I had been in France for three years and the army for four,
and I didn't want to go to the Rhine.
I wanted to get the hell hoome out of there."*
W.B. Frame, 49th Battalion
CBC, In Flanders Fields
Episode 16, "Victory"

(Above) Canadian occupation troops pose in front of the Bonn Bridge. The following caption is written on back of the photograph:

"Just about all of Personnel of Canadian H.Q. Signal Co. Administration Section: Signal office, clerks, telegraphists, switchboard operators - Dispatch riders - Instrument repair & air line sections - Cable Laying sections - cooks, etc. Quite a number looking up at German girls doing a sort of Can-Can dance at hotel across the street." (CWM, 19730108-026)

The original bridge was destroyed by the retreating German armies in the Second World War, in March 1945. It was rebuilt in the 1960s and christened ""Kennedy-Bruecke" in honour of assasinated US President John F. Kennedy. Like many buildings and bridges built in the 1960s around the world, this one lacks the architectural magnificance of its predecessor.

The Canadian Corps played a minor role in the occupation of Germany, only two of its four divisions actually crossing the Rhine. The other two stayed in Belgium and all divisions were withdrawn to Canada by early 1919. The era is stylized in Sir William Rothenstein's painting, "The Watch on the Rhine" (top right, CWM 19710261-0601).

In the rear areas, both before and after the Armistice, the troops entertained themselves with sports and artistic endeavours. Soldiers organized plays and concerts, normally on a divisional level. The most famous of these groups was 'The Dumbells' that later carried on as a civilian entertainment troupe. However, there were many others of less renown. Troops had to play all the female roles in their productions and some of them were excellent female impersonators. (Centre) A group of military thespians rehearses a play (CWM, CEF Album 5, 4144) while a chamber orchestra poses in Cologne (CWM, CEF Album 5, 4154).

The Halifax dock area, now known as the Historic Properties, during a Tall Ships event.

(Right) Arthur Lismer, "Olympic with returned soldiers, Halifax, February 1919" (CWM 19710261-0001).

The so-called "dazzle" paint scheme was not a figment of Lismer's artistic eye; rather he has fairly accurately captured the camouflage style, intended to confuse the aim of attacking German submariners. Lismer was one of several members of the future Group of Seven who benefited from the generosity of Lord Beaverbrook's sponsorship of the war artists program (another was A.Y. Jackson, several of whose paintings appear elsewhere in this book). Beaverbrook hoped that the art would be displayed in Canada for future generations. That vision has only finally been realized with the opening of the new Canadian War Museum.

For many troops their adventure of the Great War began and ended at Toronto's Union Station. (Archives of Manitoba, N22568)

"The sad thing was that so comparatively few of the men who'd borne the heat and burden of winning the battles were there, and that was one of the sad things."
C.B. Price, 14th Battalion
CBC Radio, In Flanders Fields
Episode 16, "Victory"

Georges Bertin Scott, "Unveiling Vimy Ridge Monument" (CWM, 20020045-425)

Tyne Cot Cemetery near Passchendaele.

Memory serves many purposes and takes many forms, constantly changing to suit the needs of successive generations. So it has been and so it continues today with our memories of the First World War.

Some of the earliest objects of remembrance remain the most readily obvious as one travels through northwest France and Belgium: the hundreds upon hundreds of cemeteries dotting the countryside that were established to meet the very utilitarian function of interring the war dead. A measure of the scale of death is evident from the special Michelin road map that can be obtained from the Commonwealth War Graves Commission, its over-printed purple markings forming a swath nearly 50 kilometres wide from Ypres in a wide arc south to the Somme that clearly traces the scene of four years of concentrated trench warfare. Canadians are buried in a surprisingly high number of these cemeteries. In part this was due to the Commission's purpose to bury the dead near where they fell, with no discrimination as to country of origin within the Empire, and the widespread areas in which the Canadian Corps saw action throughout the British sectors. As well, many additional Canadian soldiers and airmen who died liberating the same area in the Second World War are mingled amongst their comrades from the First World War.

Hourges Cemetery near Amiens.

The cemeteries are located in a wide variety of urban and rural settings, each unique, but all sharing some common features. Most prominent are the low stone wall surrounding the site, a tall Cross of Sacrifice overlooking it, and an altar-like plinth emblazoned with the words, "THEIR NAME LIVETH FOR EVERMORE" (see photo centre left). The poet Rudyard Kipling coined the phrase, to record his grief at the loss of his own son. A small metal vault (opposite centre) is always found inset at some place in the wall. It contains books identifying the location of those buried at the site, as well as a volume for visitors to record their own thoughts. Often, inscribed somewhere else on the wall, are words to the effect that the land has been provided by the grateful host nation (inset below left). There is no separation of those interred by rank or nation or unit or faith, although certain customs in marker inscription and placement are poignant. For example, a disturbingly large number bear the simple notation, "A Soldier of the Great War, Known Unto God" (upper left). Still others bear the names of two individuals, killed together in a fashion that made it impossible to separate the remains. Where a larger group died together (such as in a mine blast), the markers are butted together with no space between them. In places where original burials were disturbed by some later conflict, their headstones are grouped separately near a wall, each bearing the added notation, "Known to be buried near here" (upper right).

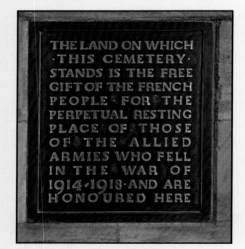

The common design elements of typical Commonwealth War Graves Commission cemeteries are clearly seen in the pictures above.

Slightly different, however, is the Zivy Crater Cemetery (right) near Vimy Ridge. Occasionally, the site of a massive loss of life is preserved and incorporated into the design of the cemetery. Here, in April 1917, 53 men were killed and their bodies buried in situ. Of the total, five were unknown and 48 were identified as having been killed in the area by the explosion of a mine. All of their names are commemorated below the cross of sacrifice.

Meeting thr immediate need of caring for remains allowed for the formal remembrance of those known to have fallen. But that left the related problem of what to do for the tens of thousands known to have died but whose remains had not been identified. Many of these certainly found a resting place as an "unknown" in one of the many cemeteries. But there remained a large number - nearly 20,000 Canadians alone - whose bodies were never recovered, either blown apart beyond recognition or lost forever in the mud and ooze of the Western Front. Each of the participating nations have built grand memorials on or near the battle sites to commemorate the heroic efforts undertaken there, and on them are recorded the names of those with no known grave. Fighting as part of the Empire forces, 6,940 Canadians are thus listed on the Menin Gate (following page), one of the large British monuments in the Ypres Salient. (The other in that area, at Tyne Cot near Passchendaele, has no Canadians listed.) Another major British memorial is at Thièpval on the Somme. Canadians who fell in that sector and elsewhere with no known grave, however, are recorded upon our own distinctive national memorials built to demonstrate the uniqueness of our contribution: Vimy Ridge, some 50 miles to the north, and Beaumont-Hamel, just down the road, for Newfoundlanders.

The Menin Gate, is one of the major memorials to British Commonwealth soldiers in the Ypres Salient. On the memorial are 54,896 names inscribed to commemorate those soldiers who died nearby and whose remains could not be identified or who are still missing. The names cover the missing and unknown between 1914 and 15 August, 1917. Others after that date are commemorated in Tyne Cot Cemetery.

Before the First World War, there was no monumental gate on the road to Menin. Two stone lions orninginally there are now in Canberra, Australia. This arch was built and finally inaugurated 24 July 1927. Each night at 8 p.m.traffic is stopped and buglers from the Ypres Fire Brigade play the Last Post and Reveille. Often visitors lay wreaths. The ceremony has been continuous since 11 November 1929, except for an interlude during the Second World War.

MENIN GATE

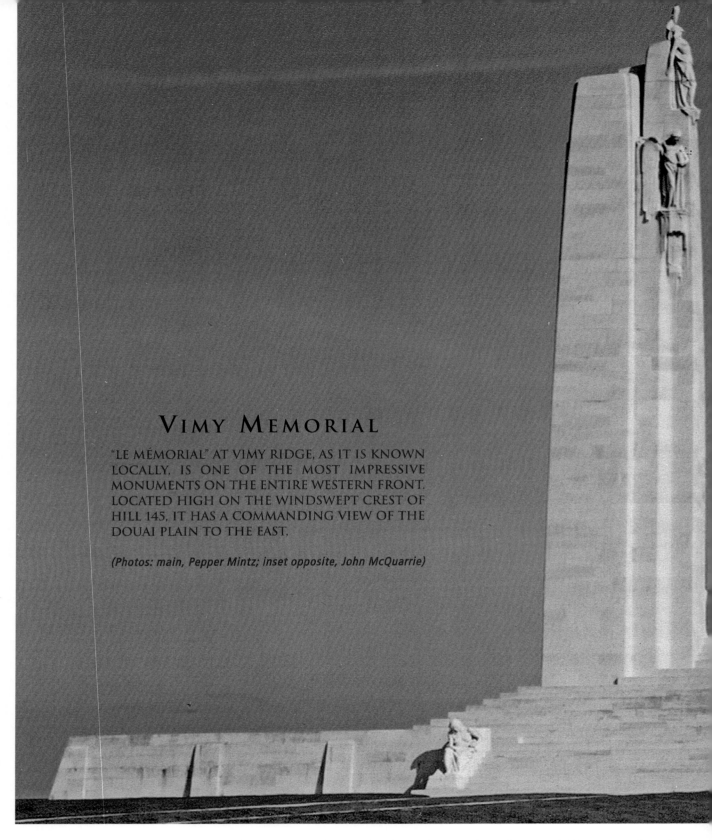

Vimy Memorial

"LE MÉMORIAL" AT VIMY RIDGE, AS IT IS KNOWN LOCALLY, IS ONE OF THE MOST IMPRESSIVE MONUMENTS ON THE ENTIRE WESTERN FRONT. LOCATED HIGH ON THE WINDSWEPT CREST OF HILL 145, IT HAS A COMMANDING VIEW OF THE DOUAI PLAIN TO THE EAST.

(Photos: main, Pepper Mintz; inset opposite, John McQuarrie)

The Vimy Memorial is staggering in it proportions, however those might be measured: overall dimensions (27 metres above its base, with the topmost figures some 110 metres above the Douai Plain); area of land covered (91.18 hectares); weight of stone (15,000 tonnes of concrete and masonry for the base; 6,000 tonnes of "trau" stone from Yugoslavia for the pylons and sculpted figures); numbers of names recorded (11,285). Although we see it today as a place of mourning, when completed in 1936, Walter Allward's design stood as the symbol of a young and dynamic nation that had contributed more than its share to victory.

The others in the series of Canadian memorials list no names, but rather serve as places of quiet contemplation marking the most famous battlefields of the Canadian Corps. The reader will have noted their prominence throughout this book: St Julien, Hill 62 and Crest Farm in the Ypres Salient area; Courcelette near the Somme; Le Quesnel, Dury and Bourlon Wood of the final Hundred Days.

THE BROODING SOLDIER

The Canadian Battlefield Memorials Commission, established in 1920, intended that a single design be repeated at all eight sites (that is, including also Vimy Ridge), but Allward's submission was judged to be "of such individuality and complexity that its character precludes it from the possibility of repetition." It was chosen to mark only Vimy Ridge where the Canadian Corps first fought as a unit.

The close runner-up by Regina sculptor Frederick Clemesha, the Brooding Soldier at St Julien, was selected for the scene of Canada's first major action at the Second Battle of Ypres. The remaining six memorials are simple inscribed blocks in park-like settings landscaped with native Canadian flora. There are four additional Newfoundland memorials that are miniature versions of that at Beaumont-Hamel, located at Courtrai in Belgium, and Gueudecourt, Monchy-le-Preux and Masnières in France).

Other nationalities have built cemeteries with slightly different design characteristics.

The French cemetery at Notre Dame de Lorette (above left) near Vimy Ridge is one of the largest national military cemeteries. French cemeteries feature the use of ossuaries, collection places for bones of the dead, while single graves are placed back-to-back. Soldiers of Islamic faith (mostly in regiments from African colonies) have a Muslim grave marker.

The United States offered the option to families to take their dead home. Those who wished could have the fallen buried in large, well-designed contemplative garden-like settings with evenly-spaced marble crosses or the Jewish Star of David, as visible in the large photo above of the Flanders Field American Cemetery and Memorial at Waregem, Belgium.

French and American cemeteries, like British Commonwealth cemeteries, celebrate the sacrifice of liberators and the land is the perpetual gift of the resident country.

German cemeteries are less conspicuous and smaller in geographic size, often containing large numbers of soldiers' remains. Within walled and often heavily treed enclosures, they often seem to have a sense of foreboding. Most graves are multiple resting places and the use of mass graves with stone markers is common. Many German cemeteries have plain yet moving sculptures as a focal point. The cemetery at the right contains 44,000 German dead and is at the village of Langemarck, near Ypres. Many of the dead are from the First Battle of Ypres in 1914.

In the archival photo below, a commemorative cross marks the smaller grave markers of Privates Sweeney, Coetzee and O'Keefe of the Princess Patricia's Canadian Light Infantry who were killed 9 May 1915, at the battle of Frezenberg Ridge just east of Ypres near the Bellewaarde Lake area. The PPCLI was not fighting with the Canadians at this time, having been sent to Flanders earlier as part of the British 27th Division. The regiment later moved back under Canadian command when Second Division was formed.

These three graves would have been battlefield burials and recorded by the unit for later recovery. Soldiers killed in action were normally buried in their blanket or gas cape. Sometimes part of their equipment or personal items might be buried with them, depending upon how hurried the burials were.

Special graves registration units would record the locations of the graves reported by the unit. Later, the bodies in battlefield sites would be collected and re-interred in collection cemeteries administered eventually by the Commonwealth War Graves Commission. Some cemeteries were more orderly from their inception, particularly around the area of medical units or rear areas. Occasionally, some soldiers would be buried in or adjacent to existing civilian cemeteries.

(Below) The original burial place for PPCLI Privates Sweeney, Coetzee and O'Keefe, killed in action 5 September 1915, and (left) their final resting places together still after re-burial in Ypres Reservoir Cemetery.
(CWM, CEF Album 1, 0487)

MAPLE LEAF LEGACY PROJECT

The Maple Leaf Legacy Project is an enormous endeavour aimed at procuring a photograph of each and every Canadian War Grave from the South African War (1899-1902), World War 1 (1914-18), World War II (1939-45), Korean War (1950-52) and all United Nations Peacekeeping Missions to the present day.

These photos are freely available on the project's web site. It is also hoped to have touch-screen interactive computer kiosks at prominent historical locations across the country, such as the Parliament Buildings in Ottawa, the Canadian War Museum and provincial and territorial Legislatures, so that any visitor may be able to look up a photograph of a war grave and print out a copy on the spot.

Most of the families and friends of Canada's war dead have never visited - and probably never will be able to visit - the graves of the fallen due to the distance and expense involved. While their bodies cannot be brought home, photos of the graves can be brought into the homes of all Canadians. In doing so, a virtual Canadian National War Cemetery will be created. In digital format this archive should be a permanent addition to the photographic inventory of Canada's war graves for generations to come.

The project relies solely on the kind assistance of hundreds of volunteers and sponsors around the world to get the photographs or to donate funds to help pay for the good work of the project.

The Maple Leaf Legacy Project is being being produced by Canadians, for Canadians, although with the help of people from many nations it is an initiative with a truly international component.

Project Director Steve Douglas, a native of Kitchener, Ontario, is currently based in Ypres because of the access to the majority of war cemeteries of the Western Front.

Steve Douglas at work (left) in his Ypres office with a spectacular view of the Menin Gate and (below) relating the story of the three PPCLI privates featured on the opposite page.

The Maple Leaf Legacy Project has registered charity status with the Government of Canada.
TO LEARN MORE VISIT: WWW.MAPLELEAFLEGACY.ORG

Many names of the fallen are also recorded in Canada in a variety of forms. Hundreds of cenotaphs, plaques and stained glass windows dedicated to the memory of lost loved ones can be found throughout the land.

The Cenotaph in Winnipeg enjoys pride of place within view of Manitoba's Legislature (visible in the background). (Photos this page, Richard Gimblett)

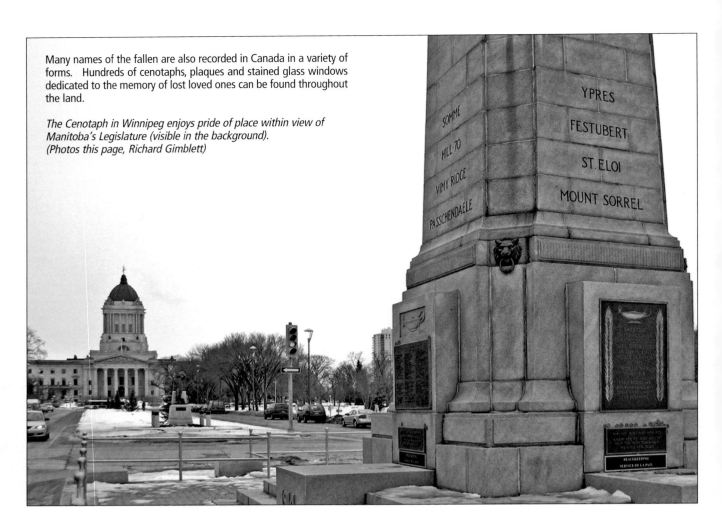

(Above left) The Olympia Hotel on Smith Street in Winnipeg was taken over in 1915 as a temporary barracks for troops of the Second Contingent. Soldiers paraded daily in front of their place of accommodation. Note the winter uniforms. (Archives of Manitoba, N22569)

Today, the hotel is the Marlborough Ramada Inn (above). The building has been renovated and the emerald green marquee restored. New floors have been added since 1915. It was here in 1925 that the Royal Canadian Legion held its founding convention, as recorded by a plaque in the lobby

Canadian Corps Cemetery, Vimy Ridge, 1917. (NAC, PA-001372)

One of the earliest memorials to the Canadian war effort was a cross commissioned by the 21st Battalion to commemorate their comrades lost in the battle for Vimy Ridge. Made of wood salvaged from the battlefield, it was erected originally in a temporary cemetery near the village of Thelus (above). After the war, it was repatriated to Kingston, Ontario from where the 21st was mobilized. Initially it was placed at the Royal Military College of Canada, but eventually the Princess of Wales' Own Regiment, as the perpetuating unit, had it mounted in the armouries (left), surrounded by the battle honours of the 21st Battalion.

(Below) The badges of every unit that formed the Canadian Expeditionary Force are painted on the fronts of the balcony in Currie Hall at the Royal Military College in Kingston, Ontario. Also at RMC stands the Memorial Arch (below left), dedicated to fallen ex-cadets.

A "drumhead" ceremony, probably the presentation of colours to a departing unit, is performed on Parliament Hill sometime after the Centre Block was destroyed by fire in 1916. The Library is clearly visible in the background. (CWM, 19940001-881)

The second level of the Peace Tower of the Parliament Buildings in Ottawa comprises a Memorial Chamber (left) to Canada's war dead. In it are the national Books of Remembrance (inset) recording the names of every Canadian who has fallen in the course of service to this country with a new page displayed every day. Quite appropriate for this modern age, a "Canada Remembers" page can be found on the website of the Department of Veterans' Affairs. It includes a digitized version of the Books of Remembrance, as well as a virtual war memorial containing selected personal memorabilia and information about the location of gravesites of fallen Canadians - both are searchable by name. The website of Library and Archives Canada (the national archives) has a link to the digitized enrolment attestation papers of every member of the Canadian Corps, again searchable by name.

(Above & left) A more recent military ceremony on Parliament Hill was the farewell by the Canadian Forces to their outgoing Commander-in-Chief, Her Excellency Governor General Adrienne Clarkson, on 21 September 2005. (Canadian Forces photo, Corporal Issa Paré)

Returning troops normally came back in formed units. At various places, they paraded before final discharge. A unit returns to Ottawa (right) and is paraded in the area of Confederation Square that is now the site of the National War Memorial. Note that the Parliament Buildings lack the Centre Block after the Great Fire of 1916 and the Peace Tower celebrating the end of the war has yet to be constructed. Crowds throng the streets and many hardy souls have found viewing positions on roofs and in windows. (CWM 19840422-056)

(Far below) The outpouring in the larger picture is repeated, in more subdued fashion, annually at Remembrance Day services at the National War Memorial in Ottawa. Despite changes in the skyline and the need to commemorate more recent wars, the War Memorial features Great War figures as symbols of Canada's military memory.

(Below) The Princess Patricia's Canadian Light Infantry marching out of Lansdowne Park to board troop trains for the front at the old downtown Ottawa Station (from the roof of which the larger photos were both taken). The unit returning from the war at right is quite possibly the same one. (NAC, CA-000200)

THE UNKNOWN SOLDIER

'He Is A Symbol Of All Sacrifice'

In Ottawa, the National War Memorial was unveiled in 1939, just in time to commemorate another world war. A significant addition to the annual Remembrance Day ceremony in the year 2000, as a Millennium Project, was the placement at the front of the War Memorial of a specially designed sarcophagus to serve as our national Tomb of the Unknown Soldier.

The following is a portion of the eulogy delivered by Governor General Adrienne Clarkson during the Interment of The Unknown Soldier at the National War Memorial on 28 May 2000:

It is a frightening thing for human beings to think that we could die and that no one would know to mark our grave, to say where we had come from, to say when we had been born and when exactly we died. In honouring this unknown soldier today, through this funeral and this burial, we are embracing the fact of the anonymity and saying that because we do not know him and we do not know what he could have become, he has become more than one body, more than one grave. He is an ideal. He is a symbol of all sacrifice. He is every soldier in all our wars.

Our veterans who are here with us today, know what it is to have been in battle and to have seen their friends cut down in their youth. That is why remembrance is so necessary and yet so difficult. It is necessary because we must not forget and it is difficult because the pain is never forgotten.

Wars are as old as history. Over 2000 years ago, Herodotus wrote: "In peace, sons bury their fathers; in war, fathers bury their sons." Today, we are gathered together as one, to bury someone's son. The only certainty about him is that he was young. If death is a debt we all must pay, he paid before he owed it.

We do not know whose son he was. We do not know his name. We do not know if he was a MacPherson or a Chartrand. He could have been a Kaminski or a Swiftarrow. We do not know if he was a father himself. We do not know if his mother or wife received that telegram with the words "Missing In Action" typed with electrifying clarity on the anonymous piece of paper. We do not know whether he had begun to live his life as a truck driver or a scientist, a miner, a teacher, a farmer or a student. We do not know where he came from.

Was it the Prairies whose rolling sinuous curves recall a certain kind of eternity?
Was he someone who loved our lakes and knew them from a canoe?
Was he someone who saw the whales at the mouth of the Saguenay?
Was he someone who hiked in the Rockies or went sailing in the Atlantic or in the Gulf Islands?
Did he have brown eyes?
Did he know what it was to love someone and be loved back?
Was he a father who had not seen his child?
Did he love hockey? Did he play defence?
Did he play football? Could he kick a field goal?
Did he like to fix cars? Did he dream of owning a Buick?
Did he read poetry?
Did he have freckles?
Did he think nobody understood him?
Did he just want to go out and have a good time with the boys?

ANCIENNE SEPULTURE D'UN
SOLDAT CANADIEN INCONNU
MORT AU COURS DE LA
PREMIERE GUERRE MONDIALE.
IL A ETE EXHUME
LE 25 MAI 2000
ET IL REPOSE MAINTENANT AU
MONUMENT COMMEMORATIF
DE GUERRE DU CANADA
A OTTAWA.

THE FORMER GRAVE OF AN
UNKNOWN CANADIAN SOLDIER
OF THE FIRST WORLD WAR.
HIS REMAINS WERE REMOVED
ON 25 MAY 2000 AND NOW
LIE INTERRED AT THE
NATIONAL WAR MEMORIAL
IN OTTAWA CANADA.

A SOLDIER
OF THE GREAT WAR
A CANADIAN REGIMENT

A SOLDIER
OF THE GREAT WAR
A CANADIAN REGIMENT

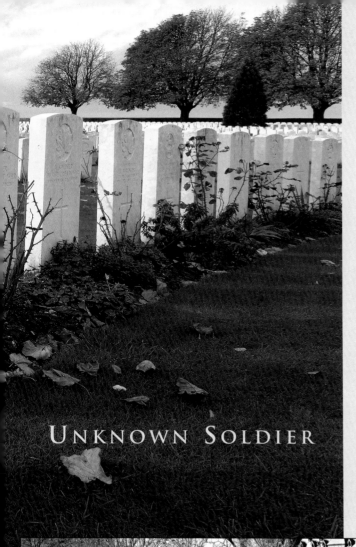

UNKNOWN SOLDIER

At the instigation of the Royal Canadian Legion, and with the assistance of the Commonwealth War Graves Commission, the remains of an unidentified Canadian soldier were repatriated from the Cabaret-Rouge Cemetery at Souchez, France, near Vimy Ridge. The original headstone from the cemetery now is on display in the Canadian War Museum, situated such that a shaft of light will shine upon it at 11 o'clock each 11 November (below left). In its place in Cabaret-Rouge stands a new headstone, recording notice of the transfer (left).

Closing remarks at the eulogy for the Unknown Soldier delivered by Governor General Adrienne Clarkson on May 28, 2000.

This unknown soldier was not able to live out his allotted span of life to contribute to his country. But in giving himself totally through duty, commitment, love and honour he has become part of us forever. As we are part of him.

In recent years attendance for Remembrance Day ceremonies at the National War Memorial in Ottawa has steadily increased. In the photo below many of the 25,000 people estimated to have been on hand in 2005 continued the tradition of leaving their poppies on the tomb of the Unknown Soldier following the ceremony (below).

Here we see Second World War veteran Victor Bushe of Metcalfe, Ontario mark an eventful Remembrance day with his son, Sergeant Nigel Bushe of the RCMP, and grandson, Air Cadet Bryce Bushe who traveled from British Columbia with his father so they could spend this special day with his grandfather. Thomas Bushe, Bryce's great grandfather, enlisted in September 1914 at age 33, served with the Royal Irish Fusiliers and was wounded in the Battle of the Somme. Victor served with the North Irish Horse, Royal Armoured Corps and saw action during the Second World War in North Africa, Italy, Belgium and Germany. Sadly, Victor Bushe left us on 24 December 2005, just weeks after this photograph was taken.

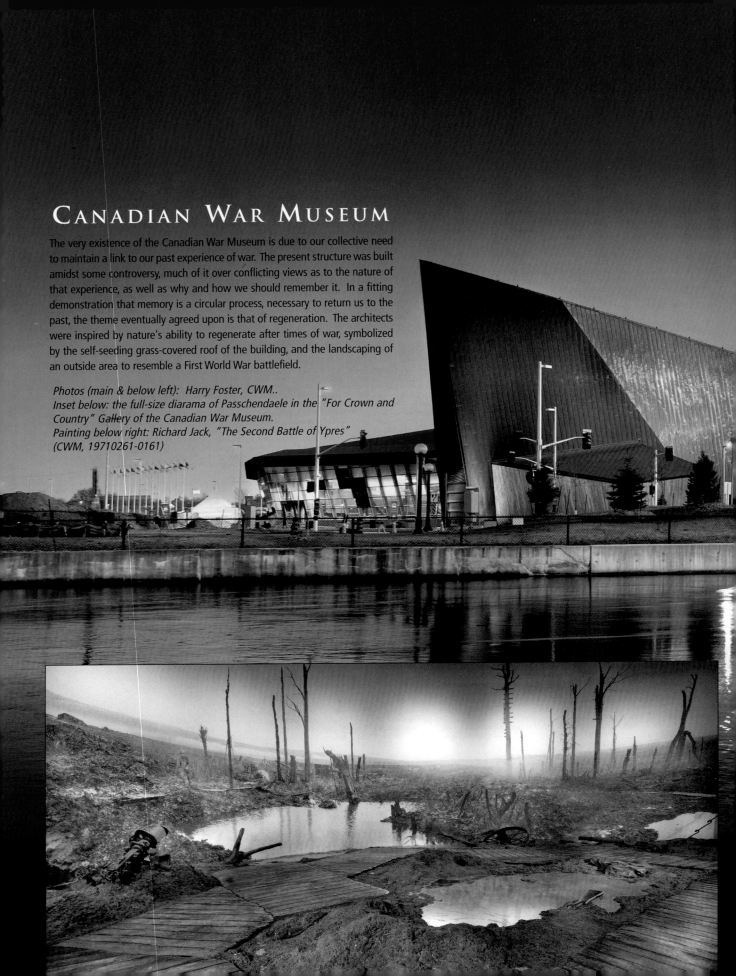

CANADIAN WAR MUSEUM

The very existence of the Canadian War Museum is due to our collective need to maintain a link to our past experience of war. The present structure was built amidst some controversy, much of it over conflicting views as to the nature of that experience, as well as why and how we should remember it. In a fitting demonstration that memory is a circular process, necessary to return us to the past, the theme eventually agreed upon is that of regeneration. The architects were inspired by nature's ability to regenerate after times of war, symbolized by the self-seeding grass-covered roof of the building, and the landscaping of an outside area to resemble a First World War battlefield.

Photos (main & below left): Harry Foster, CWM..
Inset below: the full-size diarama of Passchendaele in the "For Crown and Country" Gallery of the Canadian War Museum.
Painting below right: Richard Jack, "The Second Battle of Ypres" (CWM, 19710261-0161)

The military tourist is an essential part of this process of regeneration. There is no better way of keeping alive the memory of our fallen than by returning to the fields upon which they achieved so much, and where so many made the ultimate sacrifice. However we make the journey of retracing the footsteps of that previous generation, whether through the pages of a book or an actual visit to the sites, we help to sustain interest in the First World War.

Their name liveth for evermore.

Tyne Cot cemetery.

LANGEMARCKE
ST JULIEN
FESTUBERT
GIVENCHY

New names in
Canadian history.

More are coming –
Will you be there?

ENLIST !

C.J.Patterson

Recruiting poster, 1915. (CWM, 19900076-844)